The Seven Pillars of Catholic Spirituality

MATTHEW KELLY

BLUE
sparrow

BLUE
sparrow

THE SEVEN PILLARS OF CATHOLIC SPIRITUALITY

Copyright © 2025
Kakadu, LLC
Published by Blue Sparrow
An Imprint of Viident

Cover Design by Brady Evans
Interior Design by Faceout Studio and Maggie Barnett

ISBN: 978-1-63582-592-3 (hardcover)
ISBN: 978-1-63582-599-2 (eBook)
Audiobook available from Audible

For more information, please visit:
MatthewKelly.com

10   9   8   7   6   5   4   3   2   1

FIRST EDITION

Printed in the United States of America

Table of Contents

What If?

What if everything the Catholic Church teaches is true? This is the one question most people never consider when it comes to the Catholic faith.

Have you ever paused to consider that possibility? Not just for a fleeting moment, but really taken some time to ponder the possibility. We live in a culture that assumes that the Catholic Church's teachings are unrealistic, false, or bigoted. It's time we seriously considered the other possibility. Because if it is all true—if everything the Catholic Church teaches is true—that changes everything.

What if God really does exist and created you out of love, for a purpose and with a mission that only you can fulfill? What if Jesus Christ really did come into the world, suffer, die, and rise again to save you? What if every Mass is a miraculous encounter where bread and wine become the Body and Blood of Christ to nourish your soul and draw you closer to eternity with God?

If everything the Catholic Church teaches is true, then your life is far more extraordinary than you could ever imagine. You're not a random accident. You're a child of God, called to greatness, created for eternity. Every choice you make, every act of love, every moment of prayer matters—infinitely and forever.

What if the Catholic Church's teachings on the dignity of every human person, the sanctity of marriage, and the importance of forgiveness are not just ideals but divine truths? What if the sacraments are not just ancient rituals but deeply personal encounters with God's grace that can heal you, transform you, and guide you through life? What if Heaven is real and you are destined for it? What if God does have dreams and plans for your life that far exceed anything you could imagine for yourself?

If all of this is true, how you live your life matters. It means you are called to something greater than pleasure, comfort, and worldly accomplishment. It means your faith is not just one part of your life but the very foundation of everything.

And what if you lived as though it were all true? What if you prayed with the confidence that God hears you? What if you approached the Eucharist as the most important moment of your week? What if you loved others, forgave others, and served others believing anything you did for them, you did for Jesus in his most vulnerable moments?

If everything the Catholic Church teaches is true, then it's not just about going to Mass on Sunday, and it's not about following a set of rules.

It's an incredible gift. An incomprehensible blessing. A striking alternative to the meaninglessness secularism offers. It's an invitation to live a life of meaning and purpose, rooted in the reality of God's incredible plan for you. And the fruits of living this way are found in the lives of the saints: peace, even in the midst of chaos and turmoil; joy, even in the midst of suffering; a heart that loves deeply and aches compassionately for others; and a soul that delights in anything that is good, true, right, just, and noble.

In a culture that is dehumanizing people in a thousand different ways, Catholicism seeks to restore the very best of our humanity, ennobling us to live as children of God.

So, what if it's all true? The question isn't whether it will change your life. The question is: Are you ready to let it?

Many years ago, I was meeting regularly with a young man who was considering becoming Catholic. For three years, I answered all of his questions. Each time we met, he would bring a list of questions and objections. We would delve deep into each one, but he always returned with new objections. It seemed he was searching for reasons not to believe, rather than for reasons to believe.

Finally, I got frustrated. Not because I felt he was wasting my time, but because I felt he was wasting his time. So, this was my advice to him—and it is my advice to you today: "Live as if everything the Catholic Church teaches is true for a few months. Stop thinking about it and start living it. Live as if it were all true. That will change your life, and more importantly, it will transform you into a thoughtful, generous, wise, deeply compassionate, and loving person who is living with astounding intention."

That was seven years ago, and he has never looked back. I don't think you will either. Live as if it were all true and the fruits will speak for themselves.

You were made for more. You know it. You have more to offer. You are capable of so much more. Somewhere deep inside you know this is true. You sense it. Your intuition has never been so right. That persistent inner voice isn't lying. Listen to that voice. Don't ignore that quiet voice calling you forward. Trust that voice within and allow God to reveal your true potential.

But to awaken the God-given potential that is sleeping within you will need to acquire some new ancient habits. They may be new to you, but they have ancient origins. You may have some experience with these spiritual practices in the past, but establishing them as habits is something altogether different.

The Seven Pillars of Catholic Spirituality are ancient. But age doesn't make something less valuable or irrelevant. Our culture feels superior to anything old and infects us with a bias toward what is new. But our bias should be toward what works—and these seven spiritual habits work. This is an indisputable fact. These are the habits of the saints.

Stop wasting your life. It's time to find a new way. It's time to walk a different path. The path I propose is a well-trodden path. I wasn't the first to walk it. Faithful Catholics have been following it for centuries. It is the path that transformed my life.

It's been nearly forty years since I first set out on this path and these seven habits have enriched my life every day.

Twenty-five years ago, I wrote *Rediscover Catholicism*. What you are about to read was one part of that book. It describes the path my spiritual mentor invited me to walk in my teens, and I consider myself astoundingly blessed that by some grace I had the courage to step away from the crowd and follow his counsel.

Step by step I was taught how to establish a vibrant spiritual life. The result was a joy that defies explanation and is unlike anything the world has to offer. It is a joy that isn't dependent on fortunate circumstances. It is a joy that can coexist with sorrow, walk hand-in-hand with suffering, and sit quietly in the shadow of pain. It does not vanish in the presence of grief or uncertainty. It is a joy that reminds us that something wonderful is about to happen.

I've spent my life trying to help others experience this deep and abiding joy. I've done this by helping them establish vibrant spiritual lives in the same way I was taught. The words you are about to read are those of a hopeful twenty-seven-year-old desperate to help as many people as possible experience that same joy.

Every era is arrogant about itself in different ways. The people of this age have a tendency to look down on things that are old, and have a particular way of dismissing ancient wisdom as irrelevant to modern life. The Catholic faith has suffered at the hands of this foolishness. Many people, Catholic and not, dismiss Catholicism and its practices as irrelevant. They believe the faith has nothing to offer simply because it is old. You are about to prove that to be wildly untrue.

You hold in your hands a treasure map. Is it old? Yes. But a treasure map does not become worthless because it is old. Its value is determined by two factors: Does it lead to treasure and how great is that treasure? And I assure you this treasure map will lead you to an unimaginable bounty. You cannot even begin to conceive how different your life will be one year from now if you have the courage to live as if everything the Catholic Church teaches is true and ingrain these seven habits in your life.

Transforming people one at a time is at the heart of God's plan for the world. Are you willing to let God transform you?

Prologue

Yesterday I was visiting a friend in Atlanta. He lives in a beautiful neighborhood and as we drove past these magnificent homes, one after another, I began to ask myself, "If your spiritual life were a house, what would it be like?"

I would like to place the question before you now. If *your* spiritual life were a house, what would it be like? What street would it be on? What part of town would it be in? What would it look like? Would it be a house or a home? Is it in need of renovations? Is it peaceful, noisy, distracting, well organized, messy?

I must admit, these questions make me a little uncomfortable, but at the same time, they ignite a desire deep within me to begin the spiritual renovations that are necessary at this time in my life. Wherever you are in your spiritual journey, it is my sincerest hope that the next seven chapters will help you to begin the work you need to do on your spiritual life. Whether you are in need of a complete spiritual overhaul or some minor renovations, or you are just beginning to build your spiritual life, I hope these pages help you to begin that work.

When I read the Bible it strikes me with alarming importance that in the course of the entire Gospels, the disciples make only one request of Jesus as a group: "Lord, teach us to pray." (Luke 11:1)

The people of every age yearn for God. I yearn for God, though for the longest time I did not recognize it as such. Even now I often confuse my yearning for God with a yearning for other things and experiences. I suspect you have also come to recognize your yearning for God. We have a longing to draw nearer to God, a desire to be in communion with him.

My favorite passage from the *Catechism of the Catholic Church* appears as the first line of the first chapter, and it reads, "The desire for God is written in the human heart, because man is created by God and for God; and God never ceases to draw man to himself. Only in God will he find the truth and happiness he never stops searching for."

The request modern Catholics have of Jesus alive in the Church today is the very same request the disciples presented to the Master: "Teach us to pray."

One of the greatest tragedies of modern Catholicism is that as Catholics we are no longer considered a spiritual people. If you polled people on the streets of any city in America today and asked them to list five words to describe Catholics, I suspect only a small percentage would say *prayerful* or *spiritual*. The tragedy, however, is not how people perceive Catholics, but the possibility that the perception may reflect the reality. It is a generalization, but as Catholics in this modern climate, we tend not to take our spirituality seriously.

The seven pillars of Catholic spirituality that we will discuss in this section combine two thousand years of spiritual wisdom into a handful of spiritual exercises. They may be ancient practices, but don't let that fool you into believing that they are not relevant to your life in the modern world. These practices are dynamic and ever fresh. I don't think it is a coincidence that you find these seven pillars so common in the lives of the saints. Is it not, then, a logical and reasonable conclusion that if we apply these practices consistently to our own lives we will grow in holiness?

Every now and then we read about a natural disaster devastating a city in some part of the world with enormous waves. Watching the television footage, I am always amazed that some trees are able to withstand the wind and waves, while everything else is blown away. How do they do it? With strong, deep roots.

A tree with deep roots can weather any storm. In your life and mine it is only a matter of time before the next storm gets here: an illness, the death of a loved one, unemployment, financial difficulties, a troubled child, a natural disaster, marital strife, or any number of other things. The storms of life are inevitable. The question is not whether there will be another storm. The question is: When will the next storm get here? And when the next storm gets here, it's too late to sink the roots. When the next storm gets here, you either have the roots or you don't.

Sink these roots, the Seven Pillars of Catholic Spirituality, deep into your life and you will weather any storm. But more than that, so much more than surviving the storms of life, you will come to know the abundant life that Jesus invites us to experience here in this life and in eternity.

Our spiritual heritage is rich in wisdom and practice. If we can embrace this heritage and adapt it to the modern context, we will begin again to thrive as the spiritual people God intended us to be—individually and as a Church.

Chapter One

CONFESSION

In the 1990s I was amazed at the emergence and dominance of two great sporting legends. Michael Jordan and Tiger Woods are arguably the greatest sportsmen in history. Although these icons of modern sport may seem to have nothing to do with Catholicism, I promise you, I intend to explain the connection.

What intrigues me about the success Jordan and Woods have experienced is that the one quality that makes Michael Jordan the greatest basketball player in history is the same quality that makes Tiger Woods the greatest golfer. They play two very different sports that require very different skills and disciplines, yet their extraordinary success can be linked to a singular quality. Let me explain.

As a teenager growing up in North Carolina, Michael Jordan couldn't even make his high school basketball team, yet today he is the greatest basketball player in history. How does that happen? Some people would tell you it was mere luck or freak talent. Others would say he was in the right place and had opportunities others didn't have. Still others would suggest that he had an incredible growth spurt after high school. All of these would be wrong.

Jordan trained harder and longer in high school than anyone else on the team or on the bench. When he didn't make the team he pressed the coach for a reason. Jordan's coach explained that his free throw record was weak. So what did Jordan do? He practiced his free throw. He made five hundred free throws every day for ten years. He didn't *shoot* five hundred free throws; he *made* five hundred. He wouldn't let himself go to bed each night until he had made five hundred free throws. When would you next sleep if you didn't go to bed until you made five hundred free throws?

Jordan increased his skill and earned his place with hard work. Did he have talent? Yes. But he also worked harder to develop his talent than anybody else. When he made it to college basketball, he realized that his fadeaway jump shot was a weakness. So he focused his practice on his fadeaway jump shot until it became one of the high points of his game. By the time he entered the NBA he had mastered it—so much so that it was as if Jordan had invented the shot.

When was the last time you identified a weakness in any area of your life and then systematically set about eradicating it?

Similarly, in 1997 Tiger Woods won the Masters by a record number of strokes. In the world's most prestigious golfing event, in which young players are known for losing their nerve, the twenty-one-year-old demolished a world-class field in such fashion that many began to wonder whether golf would be competitive anymore.

Only weeks later, Woods and his coach announced at a press conference that he was going to take some time off to work on his swing. The press laughed; they thought it was a joke. Woods and his coach then proceeded to explain that they intended to completely deconstruct and reconstruct his golf swing. Baffled, the international press asked why. Woods explained that, with the help of his coach and video footage of his swing, they had discovered a flaw in his swing, which they believed would not stand up under the pressure of a tight match. Before too long, Woods returned to the tour with his new swing to completely dominate the sport like no one else in history.

Now, some people have suggested that I shouldn't speak about Tiger Woods anymore because of the struggles he has had in his personal life. And while he has certainly demonstrated a lack of character in some areas of his life, my reason for writing about him here is unchanged. I would like to be as good at being a Catholic as Tiger Woods is at playing golf. I would like you to be as well. And if Tiger Woods can teach me something about living my faith more fully, I want to learn it. I think every parish could use more parishioners who approach their practice of the faith with the discipline and commitment that Tiger Woods approaches golf with.

Both Michael Jordan and Tiger Woods have an incredible ability to look at their game and identify both their strengths and their weaknesses. Once they have done this, they work tirelessly to make their strengths impenetrable and transform their weaknesses into strengths. A world-class athlete would never even consider the idea of ignoring a weakness. World-class athletes want to know their weaknesses better than anybody else. Where did they get this idea?

Do you think it is the fruit of twentieth-century sports psychology? Do you think Michael Jordan came up with the idea and handed it on to Tiger Woods? Is it an idea that has just been born in the last twenty-five years? The answer to all of these is no.

This process of identifying strengths and weaknesses and transforming weaknesses into strengths is classic Catholic spirituality. For two thousand years, the champions of Christianity, the men and women we call saints, have been going into the classroom of silence, taking a humble and honest look at themselves, and assessing their own strengths and weaknesses. Then, armed with this knowledge, they have bravely set forth to transform their weaknesses into strengths, their vices into virtues. In the classroom of silence, they don't reflect on their basketball game or their golf swing; they reflect on their character. Their search for excellence is the most important of all: the quest for holiness and inner transformation. They understand that who we become is infinitely more important than what we do or what we have.

What are your weaknesses? Do you know? Most people don't want to know. We don't want to think about our weaknesses. We don't want to talk about them, and we certainly don't want anyone else to point them out. This is a classic sign of mediocrity, and this mediocrity has a firm grip on the Church and humanity at this moment in history. The proof is our collective attitude and approach toward Confession, and most people's inability or unwillingness to admit when they are wrong and then apologize. Great men and women want to know their weaknesses. They see those weaknesses as the key to a richer, more abundant future. Wouldn't you rather have God deal with your weaknesses in private than have them dealt with in public?

Your weaknesses are the key to the unimaginable bigger future that God has envisioned for you. Your strengths are probably already bearing all the fruit they can. They will continue to bear those good fruits in your life, but at some point they will begin to plateau. Your richer, more abundant future is intimately linked to your weaknesses.

In order to understand, imagine you are a farmer with one thousand acres of land. Five hundred acres is producing wonderful fruit and an abundant harvest. You have a variety of crops and a small orchard of fruit trees. But the other five hundred acres is completely neglected. This land is overrun with weeds; there are rocks in the field and a couple of abandoned old cars that have grass growing up through them.

Now consider how you want your future to be bigger than your past. You cannot plant your crops an extra time each year. The first five hundred acres is already producing all the fruit it is capable of producing. You could slave on the first five hundred acres and squeeze a little more out of it, increasing the crop size by a fraction. And if that were the only five hundred acres, I would encourage that. But that is not the pathway to your bigger future.

If you genuinely want to build that bigger future, you need to get into that neglected second five hundred acres of land and transform it into producing land. You need to get those old cars out of the field and remove the rocks. You need to pull out the weeds and till the soil. In this way you can almost double the harvest that you are producing.

The first five hundred acres is your strengths. Our culture obsesses over these and encourages us to focus on these alone. But that is because our culture does not have a vision for the human person. The culture has no interest in you becoming whole. Far from wanting you to become the-best-version-of-yourself, the culture is driven by productivity and consumption. To the culture, you are just a consumer and a cog in the global economic wheel. But God has a much greater vision for you. And it is for this reason that he gently encourages you to explore that other five hundred acres of your farm—your weaknesses.

More than that, God wants to get down in the dirt with you. He wants to work with his children. God is willing to do all the heavy lifting. He yearns for our cooperation, but he will not go where he is not invited.

It is this second five hundred acres that we come to Confession to explore and begin to work on.

• Turning to God •

I have spent much of my adult life speaking to groups around the world about the Seven Pillars of Catholic Spirituality. One of the questions I am asked most often is, "Why do you put Confession first?" Others will say, "You should let people warm up and get comfortable before you drop Confession on them." But there is a reason I placed Confession as the first of the seven pillars.

When John the Baptist first appeared in the desert of Judea, this was his message: "Repent, prepare the way of the Lord." (Matthew 3:2) Later, when Jesus began his ministry, he led with this message: "Repent, for the kingdom of heaven is at hand." (Matthew 4:17)

Repent is a powerful word. But what does it mean for you and me, here and now, more than two thousand years later? It means the same as it did to the people walking around the dusty pathways in their sandals, trying to inch closer to Jesus as he passed through their town or village. *Repent* means "to turn back to God."

I find myself needing to turn back to God many times a day, in ways small and large. It is not a matter of guilt and it is not a shameful thing. It is simply that at his side I am a better person—a better son, husband, father, brother, friend, employer, and citizen. Over time, I have also come to realize, quite painfully, that when I turn away from God I am also turning my back on my true self. Do you need to turn back to God today? Do you need to repent?

If we are honest with ourselves, if we can stomach a moment of truth, if we are willing to give truth a place in our lives above all our excuses and justifications, I think each of us discovers for ourself that we need to turn back to God. We often turn away from God, sometimes in small ways, just for a moment, and at other times in much larger ways. Turning our backs on God is an inner action. It is quite possible for people to turn their backs on God and still go to church every Sunday. The external actions don't guarantee the internal disposition. Have you turned your back on God?

Very few people turn their backs to God completely. Most of us just turn our backs on him in one or two areas of our lives. Most of us turn our backs on God in one corner of our hearts. In what area of your life have you turned your back on God?

Every journey toward something is a journey away from something. If we need to turn back to God at this moment in our lives, we also need to turn away from whatever led us away from God and keeps us away. It may be that certain people have led you to stray from God—perhaps possessions have distracted you from your true and authentic self, or maybe pleasure has seduced you into walking a wayward path. Whatever has distracted you, it is important to realize that you cannot journey to a new place and at the same time stay where you are. This is why Confession is first. Walking with God demands that we bring order to our lives and put first things first. Sometimes it is just as important to know what you are journeying away from as it is to know what you are journeying toward.

The journey toward the-best-version-of-yourself is a journey away from the defects of the-present-version-of-yourself. The question that really presents itself to you, me, and this modern age collectively is: Are we willing to turn back to God? Are you willing to be more attentive to what God is calling you to be?

If you are, I think you will find that Catholic spirituality is rich with tools and insights that are astoundingly helpful. If you are willing to pursue truth wherever it leads you, I know you will discover there is genius in Catholicism. But it is not always apparent on the surface. You have to delve into it. I hope you will.

• I Am a Sinner •

Every day I find myself doing things that are self-destructive and that make me a lesser person. I say things that hurt others, or I hurt others by not saying things. When that happens, you can be sure the things I am thinking are giving birth to those words and actions. These are the thoughts, words, and actions that deviate from the natural order and separate me from the peace of knowing I am contributing positively to the common good of the unfolding universe.

The strange thing is, deep within I don't want to think, say, and do these things. I don't want to be the lesser person; I want to be the-best-version-of-myself. I want to live by contributing to other people's happiness, not their misery. In each moment of each day, I find myself caught in a struggle. I am divided. No different from you, I find myself experiencing what Paul described: "The good that I would I do not, and the evil that I would not it is that which I do." (Romans 7:19)

I am a sinner and I need to be saved. I need to be saved from myself and from my sin. There are many people who love me deeply—parents, siblings, friends, colleagues, and neighbors—but they cannot save me. I need a savior. It is the clarity of this realization that is life changing. This is what makes me eligible for membership in the Catholic Church. Jesus didn't come for the healthy; he came for the sick, and he established the Church to continue his work (cf. Mark 2:17). I am imperfect, but I am capable of change and growth. We are all imperfect but perfectible. The Church holds me in my weakness, comforts me in my limitations, endeavors to heal me of my sickness, and nurtures me back to full health, making me whole again. And throughout this process, the Church manages to harness all my efforts and struggles, not only for my own good, but for the good of the entire Church and indeed humanity. This is just a tiny part of the incredible mystery of the Church.

• The Drama of Life •

Since my late teens I have been speaking and writing extensively about what I like to call "the journey of the soul." In *The Rhythm of Life,* I described it as a journey from point A to point B, with point A representing the person you are today and point B representing all God created you to be (the-best-version-of-yourself). The great spiritual North Star is God's unchanging invitation to holiness. Point B is where you experience an intimate union with God. This journey is the adventure of salvation. The whole drama of a person's life can be understood by examining the tension between the-person-I-am and the-person-I-ought-to-be. This is the tension of life. And it is the resolution of this tension that Paul spoke of when he suggested we must each work out our salvation (cf. Philippians 2:12).

Everything has its meaning in relation to the goal, and when we forget the goal, nothing makes sense. When we forget that God wants us to live holy lives, we become disoriented. When we lose sight of the great spiritual North Star, we become lost and confused. This is why Catholicism means so little to so many today, because they have forgotten—or in some cases have never been introduced to—the goal of the Christian life.

Everything should be weighed with the journey in mind and the goal in sight. The question that should be a consistent part of our inner dialogue is, "Will what I am about to do help me to become the-best-version-of-myself?"

This is the drama of life—the struggle to become the-best-version-of-myself, the quest to bridge the gap between the-person-I-am and the-person-God-calls-me-to-be and created me to be.

• A Sacred Encounter •

It is within this context that I wish to speak to you about the beauty and genius of the practice of Confession. In my own personal journey, Confession has played a very powerful role, helping me to strive to become the-best-version-of-myself. I find Confession to be a humbling experience, but not a humiliating one. Above all, I find that it is an experience of liberation that enables me to reassess where I am in the journey, helps me to identify what is holding me back, and encourages me to continue along the way. The sacrament of Reconciliation is much more than just confessing our sins and asking for forgiveness (though that in itself can be tremendously powerful both spiritually and psychologically). Confession is an integral part of the genius of Catholicism, which seeks to nurture the whole person and transform the entire world into a place where all men and women can live in the peace and joy of God.

While any spiritual exercise can be helpful in our journey, I find regular Confession to be a particularly powerful tool. As I have traveled the world, it has become apparent that this sacrament has been abandoned during our own time. I believe this has happened because a tragic mediocrity has gripped the Church.

People striving to excel in any area of life want to know their weaknesses so they can work to overcome them. This striving for excellence is precisely what needs to be re-ignited in Catholics today. Confession is the perfect spiritual practice to rekindle our passion for excellence in the spiritual life.

When I close my eyes in prayer, I see the-person-I-am and the-best-version-of-myself side by side, and I am challenged to change. This is what takes place in Confession. We prepare by asking ourselves some soul-searching questions in an examination of conscience. Those questions give birth to the dual vision of the person we are at this moment and the person we are capable of becoming. We then bring our faults, failings, and flaws to God. Through this process we open ourselves up to God and the mysterious gift of grace. This grace often takes the form of a stronger desire to become a-better-version-of-ourselves.

Grace is the power of God alive within us. It heals the wounds that our sins have created and helps us to maintain moral balance. Grace helps us to persevere in the pursuit of virtue. It enlightens our minds to see and know which actions will help us become all God has created us to be. Grace inspires us to love what is good and shun what is evil. Grace is not a magical illusion. It is mystical and real.

I come to this sacrament to reconcile with myself, with God, and with the community. Confession is not just a cleansing experience; it is also a strengthening experience. Confession is an opportunity for you and God to work together to form a-better-version-of-yourself. It also increases our desire for holiness, and that is a desire we should fan with all our energy.

• Common Objections •

There are, of course, some common objections to the practice of Confession. The secular culture propagates the myth that there is no such thing as sin or evil, no objective truth, and no universal right and wrong. They tell us that these are just ideas the Church invented to control and manipulate people. I assure you, sin and evil are real. This truth should require no proof or explanation. If you feel it does, turn on your television tonight and watch the evening news, or take a casual walk through history.

This idea is strengthened by the fact that most people don't identify with sin because we see ourselves and others as generally good. This allows us to overlook the deeply rooted nature of sin in our attitudes, our habitual ways of thinking, and our orientation to life. But Jesus did not come simply to heal us of our external behaviors. He wants to reorient our attitudes, behaviors, and the way we think. Sin is obvious in the external actions of humanity throughout history, but beyond our external behaviors it is also deeply psychological and emotional.

Once we consciously recognize that sin and evil exist in our world, we are faced with the problem of history: What do we do about sin and evil? It would be lovely if we could gather up all the evil people and put them together on one island, leaving them to self-destruct in their collective sinfulness. That is not possible because the line that separates good from evil is not out there somewhere. This line does exist, but not with some people on one side and others on the other side. The line that separates good from evil is cast down the center of my heart and yours; the battle is within. So the question is, are we willing to fight the battle?

The secular view of sin and evil seems almost absurd the moment it is removed from the self-centered, pleasure-seeking environment that sustains and encourages it. The objections of our non-Catholic Christian brothers and sisters to the practice of Confession require considerably more discernment.

The catchcry of modern Christians has become, "I don't need to confess my sins to a priest. I can confess them straight to God." You *can* do anything you want; that is the nature of the freedom with which God endows us. But if you are serious about being Christian, then it follows that you are serious about seeking and doing the will of God.

The tradition of Confession is deeply rooted in the life and teachings of Jesus, as seen in the Gospels. I have often wondered how non-Catholic Christians are able to ignore or explain away some of these central passages; for example, John's account of Pentecost: "'Peace be with you. As the Father has sent me, so I am sending you.' And when he had said this, he breathed on them and said, 'Receive the Holy Spirit. Whose sins you forgive are forgiven them, and whose sins you retain are retained.'" (John 20:21–23)

But perhaps the biggest danger with the direct-to-God approach is that it becomes all too easy to deceive ourselves, and then we begin to create God in our image. When it is "just me and God" it is all too easy to project my own qualities and biases upon God. Then, rather than being created in the image of God, we begin to create God in our own fallen image.

There are two truths of self-knowledge for us to consider here. The first is that as human beings we all have an incredible ability to deceive ourselves. The second is that we almost never see things as they really are.

We all think we have 20/20 vision in most things, but it simply is not the case. To prove this point I often ask groups at seminars and retreats to write down on a small piece of paper whether they think they are an average, above-average, or below-average driver. More than eighty percent of participants consider themselves to be above-average drivers. However, the statistical reality suggests that this is not possible. So, we are presented with two options: Either some of us don't see our driving ability as it really is, or my seminars attract a disproportionate number if above-average drivers. I think we all know which it is.

We almost never see things as they really are. When I go to Confession, half the time I need the priest to say, "You are being too easy on yourself." The other half of the time, I need him to say, "You are being too hard on yourself." I almost never see things as they really are. This is just one small part of the genius of Confession.

Excellence in any field requires coaching. Coaches see things we don't, and they are able to hold us accountable. I remember once I had my golf swing recorded. When I went home and watched it on my television I couldn't believe that was my golf swing. In my mind my swing was smooth and graceful. In reality—and recordings don't lie—it was quite erratic. Just like I needed coaching in golf and tennis as a child when I was keen to excel, I need spiritual coaching. I am so grateful for all the priests who have given their lives to provide us with invaluable spiritual coaching. Who is your spiritual coach?

A similar dynamic exists in our relationships. God gives us husbands and wives, brothers and sisters, parents, colleagues, and friends to help us to see things as they really are. And there is no relationship more precious in this world than the friendship of people we love, trust, and respect enough to allow them to correct us when we are not seeing things as they really are. We need to be constantly mindful of our ability to deceive ourselves and our tendency to distort the way we see things in our relationship with God and our relationships with others.

Today, many Catholics subscribe to the Protestant and Evangelical view that they don't need to confess to a priest. I will point out that while many Catholics claim the *right* to confess directly to God, my research suggests that, unlike many of our non-Catholic brothers and sisters, Catholics who use this argument tend not to be in the habit of confessing directly to God either. Too often it is used not to justify a different form of confession, but as an excuse to avoid confession altogether.

Another objection that has been raised is that Confession (or Reconciliation, as it is known in some parts of the world now) was only instituted in 1215 at the Fourth Lateran Council, and therefore was not part of Christian tradition from the beginning. This is clearly not the case. While the earliest Christian writings, such as *The Didache,* from the first century, are not clear on the form or procedure to be used for the forgiveness of sins, in the second century Father Irenaeus makes it clear in his writings that the sacrament goes back to the beginning of the Church. Christian writers of the third and fourth centuries such as Origen, Cyprian, and Aphraates clarify that confession is to be made to a priest, and we have no reason to believe that this was not the practice from the beginning. In *Leviticum Homiliae,* which was written around 244, Origen refers to the person who "does not shrink from declaring his sin to a priest of the Lord." Seven years later, in *De Lapsis,* Cyprian writes, "Finally, of how much greater faith and more salutary fear are they who . . . confess to the priests of God in a straightforward manner and in sorrow, making an open declaration of their conscience." Writing to advise priests, Aphraates says in *Demonstrationes,* "If anyone uncovers his wound before you, give him the remedy of repentance. And he that is ashamed to make known his weakness, encourage him so that he will not hide it from you. And when he has revealed it to you, do not make it public."

The Fourth Lateran Council didn't invent the practice of Confession as we know it today. The Council sought only to reaffirm what it understood to have been the constant practice of Christians since the beginning, and to emphasize the advantages of this practice for all men and women who desire to draw nearer to God.

Among Catholics who still hold a place for Confession in their spiritual life, there are some who consider the practice necessary only in the case of serious sin (according to the minimum obligation set out in canon law). This argument makes me wonder what type of relationships these people have with their spouses, siblings, children, employers, colleagues, and close friends.

Let us take as our example a relationship between a husband and a wife. Would it be good for their marriage if they never apologized to each other for anything? In 1970, the movie *Love Story* was a huge hit and went on to win an Academy Award and three Golden Globes. The most famous line from the movie proclaims, "Love means never having to say you're sorry." I wonder what impact that one line has had on viewers' relationships with the people they love and their relationship with God? The screenwriter has clearly confused love with pride.

Would it be healthy for a relationship if a husband and wife apologized only for serious offenses? How healthy would your key relationships be if you never apologized? I would suggest that they would not be healthy at all; rather, they would be massively dysfunctional and woefully inadequate. I also suspect that we all know at least one person who refuses to apologize—ever—for anything. Even when it is blatantly obvious that this person has done some wrong, filled with pride, he or she stubbornly refuses to apologize. Sometimes these people will not even admit any wrongdoing. Do you see God in them? Are they the light in the darkness? Do they represent hope and goodness to everyone around them? Are they becoming the-best-version-of-themselves?

If we apply this guidance of never apologizing to our relationship with God, that relationship will suffer the fate that so many modern human relationships are suffering.

After the cultural objections and non-Catholic Christian objections, there are, of course, Catholic objections and excuses. People say to me all the time, "I cannot go to Confession with my priest." When I ask them why, they reply, "Because he knows me." The priest is supposed to know you. It helps that he knows you. The more he knows you, the more helpful he can be to you in your inner journey. You don't go to a different doctor every time you are sick. Your doctor knows you—your medical history, your allergies, and the circumstances of your life. All this makes him or her infinitely more effective. Similarly, you can go to Confession with a priest who does not know you, or you can go to a different priest every time, but there is an additional advantage to having a regular confessor: Because he knows you and the various aspects of your life, he is able to provide unique insight and continuity to the experience.

Others will say, "I couldn't go to Confession to a priest I know." When again I ask why, they reply, "Oh, if he knew my sins he would never talk to me again." This is absurd. When we reveal our faults and failings, most people don't love us less; they love us more. Besides, it is not as if you are going to tell him anything he has not heard before. You are not that original. The ways men and women sin are remarkably unoriginal and similar.

One thing that we have lost sight of is that the priest is there to help you become the-best-version-of-yourself. He has given his whole life to serve the people of God, so at that moment the only thing he is concerned with is helping you in your journey to become all God created you to be. He may not say it in this way, but as you approach the experience of Confession keep in mind that everything the priest says is designed to help you live a life of holiness.

These represent the common objections that the people of our present age have toward the Catholic experience of Confession. But with all that said, I would like to affirm once again that God is not an unjust dictator trying to rule humanity with an iron fist. God doesn't want to control or manipulate you, he doesn't want to force you to do things you don't want to do, and he doesn't want to make you feel guilty and bad about yourself. God wants you to become the-best-version-of-yourself, and in turn he sends you out into the world to help others to do the same. We all have faults and failures, and we all have inner tensions. Prayer, the Sacraments, and the Scriptures are all wonderful gifts designed to help us to understand and manage our inner tensions and take one step closer to God each day.

• Behold the Beauty •

We all have spiritual disease. We all have sins. Some people like to pretend that they don't, but over time their sins spread through their lives like cancer in the body. Like cancer, if our sin is not addressed and arrested, in the end it will devour us. Other people try to justify their sins with all types of explanations, none of which will ever satisfy their own hearts. Then there are those who go to "experts" with the hope that such people will help them overcome their troubled consciences.

The truth is, I do things every day that are contrary to the ways of God, things that stop me from being the-best-version-of-myself, and so do you—every day. Then we carry all this baggage around with us and it affects us in ways that we are often not even aware of. Our sins affect us physically, emotionally, intellectually, spiritually, and psychologically. They affect our relationships, our work, our health, our intellectual clarity, and our ability to genuinely embrace and experience all of life. Sin limits our future by chaining us to the past. Yet, most people are able to convince themselves either that sin doesn't exist, that they don't sin, or that their sins are not affecting them. But if we take an honest inventory of our thoughts, words, and actions, it becomes abundantly clear that every one of us does things that are self-destructive, offensive to others, contrary to the natural laws of the universe, and in direct conflict with the ways of God. If we really think we can carry all this around inside us and that it is not affecting us, then we are only deceiving ourselves.

If you want to spend the rest of your life arguing for your weaknesses, so be it. If you want to keep losing your temper and telling yourself, "it's my character," go ahead. If you want to have someone try to explain away or justify the sins of your life, go to a psychologist or a psychiatrist. But if you want peace in your heart, I want to personally invite you to come to Confession. There is no treasure in life like a clear conscience. If you want the joy of a clear conscience, come to Confession.

The mystery of grace can never be adequately described by cold words on cold pages. It must be experienced. So if you haven't been to Confession for a while, maybe now is your time. Perhaps it has been ten years, or twenty years, maybe even longer. Jesus says to you, "Do not be afraid." (Matthew 14:27) Bring the sins of your life and place them at the feet of Jesus in this sacrament of Reconciliation. Do not think of it as confessing your sins to a priest; think of it as confessing your sins to God your heavenly Father.

God sees your unrealized potential. He sees not only who you are but also who you can be. Ask him to share that vision with you.

Our faults and failings have a tendency to eat away at us inside, but great freedom is born from bringing our darkness into the light. Darkness cannot survive in the light. While we hide our faults and failings, they grow larger and develop a power over us. Before we know it, we are planning our days around our self-destructive habits, much like an alcoholic plans his day around when he will drink. And the more we try to hide these faults and weaknesses, the more power they tend to have over us. If they are serious enough and left unattended for long enough, they can begin to control our whole lives. But when we bring them into the light, they lose their power over us.

I assure you, if you approach this sacrament with a sincere and humble heart, you will experience the flow of grace in your life. Listen to those words of absolution: "By the ministry of the Church, may God grant you pardon and peace, and I absolve you from all your sins in the name of the Father, and of the Son, and of the Holy Spirit. Amen." As the priest speaks these words the floodgates of grace are opened and your soul will be filled with a deep peace. You will experience an inexplicable lightness and an intoxicating sense of joy and liberation.

Confession is a gift. Behold the beauty. Embrace the treasure.

• Self-Knowledge •

In the spiritual life, it is very important to grow not only in our knowledge and understanding of God but also in knowledge and understanding of ourselves. Both knowledge of God and knowledge of self are necessary to make the journey of the soul. These two are inextricably linked, and one without the other is useless.

Confessing our sins in the sacrament of Reconciliation helps us to develop this self-knowledge. The saints hungered for it. They developed it from hours of self-examination and consistent practice of Confession. They knew their strengths and weaknesses, their faults, failings, and flaws, their talents and abilities, their needs and desires, their hopes and dreams, their potential and their purpose. They were not afraid to look at themselves as they really were by the light of God's grace in prayer. They knew that the things of this world are passing, and that when this brief life is over, we will each stand naked in the presence of God. At that moment, money, power, status, possessions, and worldly fame will mean nothing. The only thing that has value in that moment is character—the light within you. Who we become is infinitely more important than what we do or what we have. As

Francis of Assisi once said, "Remember, you are what you are in the eyes of God, and nothing else."

Get to know yourself. The gifts of self-knowledge include freedom from the world's image of who you are (and who you should be) and an unquenchable compassion for others. The more I get to know myself (and my own brokenness), the more I am able to accept and love others. Furthermore, the more I get to know myself and my sinfulness, the more I am able to understand others and be tolerant of their faults, failings, flaws, addictions, and brokenness. Self-knowledge breeds the ultimate form of compassion.

Self-knowledge also deflates all the false pride and egotism in our lives. Genuine self-knowledge is humbling, and two humble people will always have a better relationship than two prideful people. Not sometimes. Always.

Get to know yourself and every relationship in your life will improve.

• A New Habit •

Our lives change when our habits change. I have been convinced of the power of the habit of regular Confession in my own life, and I would like to encourage you to make it a spiritual habit in your life.

Is once a year during Lent enough? Well, it's enough to fulfill your obligation, but that would be minimalism. Becoming the-best-version-of-yourself and loving God are not about obligations and minimalism. When we are dedicated to these matters our aspirations soar far beyond the rules and regulations of our faith. These rules and regulations define only the lower limits of our quest, but God invites us to explore the optimum possibilities.

Consider this analogy. How often do you wash your car, or have it washed? Perhaps once every two or three weeks, maybe once a month, but it is probably not ten years since you had your car washed! And when your car is all shiny and clean on the outside and clean and tidy on the inside, you feel pretty good about that. Driving a clean car feels different than driving a dirty car.

When you are driving home from the car wash with your clean car, what do you pray? You pray it doesn't rain, right? Or you at least think it, hope it! As if God doesn't have better things to worry about. There are fifty thousand people dying every day in Africa from extreme poverty and preventable disease, but you just got your ten-dollar car wash and you want that at the top of his list. In any event, it doesn't rain, but the next day you are driving down the road and there is a big puddle of mud right in the middle. What do you do? You go around it, of course; you just got your car washed.

The day after that you think to yourself, *It might get cold later; I better take a jacket.* You take a jacket with you but you don't need it. So you say to yourself, *I'll put this in the backseat; I'll get it later.* Do you get it later? No. The next day you think to yourself, *I have to go to the doctor today; I better take a book or a magazine with me, because they never seem to have any good magazines.* Besides, what type of people go to a doctor's office? That's right, sick people. Then they all gather together in a little room with six magazines and they touch those magazines with their sick fingers. When you get to the doctor's you pick up that magazine and look at the cover and it reads, "Issue 137, February 1983," and you think to yourself, *How many sick people have been here since February 1983?* You bring your own magazine and once you get done with your doctor's visit you put that magazine on the backseat of your car. You say to yourself, *I'll get it later.* But you don't.

The next day you are going somewhere and it's getting late, you are hungry, and you don't know when you are going to have a chance to eat. So you go to the drive-through and get whatever it is you get when you go to the drive-through. Now you are driving while eating, and you're talking on your cell phone, so you are steering with your knees. When you get done eating you say to yourself, *I won't put this trash on the backseat; I just got my car washed.* So you get all the trash from the meal and you stuff it back into the bag the food came in and say to yourself, *I'll just put this trash neatly on the floor in the backseat. I'll get it out as soon as I get home.* Do you? Probably not.

The following day you throw another little piece of junk into the backseat and the day after that you toss another piece back there. Before you know it, it's Sunday again, and you're coming home from Church, and what do you have now? That's right, you've got the bulletin, which you probably read while

Father was giving his homily. So, you think to yourself, *I've already read this,* as you throw it over your shoulder into the backseat. The next day it's a gum wrapper or some other small bits of trash and the day after that it's one or two little bits of junk that you are moving from home to work or vice versa.

The next thing you know, two or three weeks have passed since you got your car washed. The car is quite messy on the inside and dirty on the outside, and you become less careful with it. You just throw another little piece of trash in the backseat because there is already so much that you won't notice the extra piece. And then, before long, you are throwing big bits of trash back there. Do you know why? Because you have lost your sensitivity, and once you lose that sensitivity a big piece of trash doesn't look that bad among all those little bits!

We lose our sensitivity to sin in exactly the same way. After a while, a big self-destructive behavior doesn't look that bad among all those little self-destructive behaviors.

When you get your car washed you are sensitive to the things that make it dirty. In the same way, after you have been to Confession you are sensitive to the things that stop you from being the-best-version-of-yourself. When you come out of Confession you are sensitive to the thoughts, words, actions, people, and places that will not help you to walk with God. I don't know how long that sensitivity lasts for you, but after a while it wears off and you become indifferent to the things that will not help you to live a life of holiness and be true to yourself.

Haven't you ever noticed the way people living good lives have a glow about them? They don't seem to be carrying the weight of the world on their shoulders. When you go to Confession your soul is cleansed and an inner beauty shines from within you. But after a few weeks, the little sins begin to pile up, and before you know it, a big sin doesn't look so bad on top of a pile of small sins. And once you add the big one to the pile, you figure you've made a mess already so you might as well really make a mess. Little by little, you begin to lose your sense of sin. Before you know it, you are very unhappy, and you don't really know why. You don't feel at peace with yourself and you find yourself becoming impatient and irritable with the people around you. You begin to experience a certain restlessness and anxiety, but you don't know what is causing it.

How long does this desensitization take? I suspect it is different for different people, and even different at various times in our lives. There have been times when I have struggled with habitual sins, even while trying to rid my life of them. During those times I have gone to Confession as often as every week. But now, at this time in my life, I lose that sensitivity after a month, so I have made a habit of going to Confession once a month. If I don't, I find I become inattentive and desensitized to the things that separate me from God, my neighbor, and my true self.

Another interesting lesson I learned is that I have to pick a specific time each month. Otherwise, one month started turning into two or three. Now I go to Confession the first weekend of each month. That way, there is no confusion and I don't open the door to procrastination, laziness, and all those other lurking traits that want to steal me away from God and my best self.

How often should you go to Confession? No one can tell you. The Church requires that you go at least once a year, but encourages regular Confession. Some people go once a week, others go once a month, and there has long been a rumor that Pope John Paul II used to confess daily.

Once a month works for me, but if you haven't been in a while, at first you may wish to go every week to reawaken your spiritual senses. This weekly Confession may be particularly helpful if you are caught in some habitual sins. But as the weeks pass, most people should be able to apply the rhythm of monthly Confession to their spiritual life.

There is still nothing quite as wonderful as a clear conscience. Nothing fills us with joy in the same way. Ah, a clear conscience—it is the ultimate simple pleasure.

• Temptation •

Once we have turned back to God and embraced him again, like the prodigal son embraced his father (cf. Luke 15:20), we still have to live in the world.

Here we face all the distractions and temptations that have drawn us away from the path of peace so many times before.

Temptation is real. Every day I am tempted to do things that do not lead me to become the-best-version-of-myself. I suspect the same is true for you. I am tempted by lust, gluttony, greed, anger, envy, laziness. . . .

It seems to me that if we can master the moment of temptation, we can master the Christian life. There should be whole books about the moment of temptation. There should be courses we can take to study it and learn how to respond to it. But we almost never talk about it.

There are some immutable truths when it comes to our struggle with temptation. The first is this: Don't dialogue with it. When temptation whispers in your ear, turn away. Temptation will say things like, "Everybody is doing it," or "It won't matter just this once," or "You deserve it," or "Nobody will know." Don't surrender the peace in your soul. Keep yourself busy. The temptation will pass. Learn to prize the peace in your soul above all else.

But it is not enough for me to advise you not to dialogue with temptation. That would be like me saying, "When you get home tonight there will be a small crystal container filled with a magical purple potion on your front doorstep. Anything you pour that purple potion on will turn instantly to solid gold—as long as while you are pouring it you don't think about a herd of purple hippopotamuses!"

You have probably never thought of a herd of purple hippopotamuses, but as soon as you go to pour that potion, what is the first thing that you are going to think about? A herd of purple hippopotamuses. As hard as you may try, you will not be able to get that image out of your mind. The same thing happens when we try not to dialogue with temptation by thinking about not dialoguing with temptation. We end up in a dialogue with temptation. What we focus on increases in our lives. We have to turn our focus away from what stops us from experiencing our full potential in Jesus and place our focus on what will cause us to experience the life Jesus invites us to in him.

It is not enough not to dialogue with temptation. We have to replace the dialogue of temptation with another type of dialogue. What do we call that other type of dialogue? Prayer. In order to overcome temptation we have to pray unceasingly in the midst of it. But the truth is, most of the time we don't pray when we are being tempted. Do you know why? Because we are people of faith! This may sound strange to many, and it may appear to be a contradiction, but let me explain.

As men and women of faith, we believe that God is all powerful. We know this instinctively, and often we don't want God and his all-powerful self getting in the way of our sins. We love some of our sins. This is the first truth we discover on the path to conversion. We love some of our self-destructive behaviors, especially the habitual ones.

It is important that we recognize and acknowledge this truth. Then, as it is with all truth, we have to respond to it. We don't have a choice; truth demands a response. We can choose how we respond, but we cannot choose not to respond. You cannot take the Fifth with truth. Once you discover it you are required to respond. You can, of course, ignore the truth you discover, but that in itself is a response.

One response may be to turn to God and beg him to free you from a certain habitual sin. Then, next time you are tempted to entertain that sin, call out to God unceasingly in prayer, asking him to deliver you from the temptation.

Another very real possibility is that you don't want to give up a certain habitual sin. If that is the case, and you genuinely have no desire to give up a certain self-destructive behavior, then I encourage you to go to church and sit in the presence of God and ask him to give you the desire to give up that sin. That prayer might sound something like this: *Lord, I know [my sin] is stopping me from becoming the-best-version-of-myself, and that it is stopping me from loving you and the people in my life. But I love this sin. Please give me the desire to give it up.* This is an honest prayer, and all true growth in the spiritual life begins with this type of raw honesty.

Temptation is real and we all experience it every day. The best way to spend your time while you are waiting for temptation to pass is to pray. Replace the dialogue of temptation with a dialogue of prayer: *God, I know what is good and true, but I am still attracted to what is self-destructive. Give me strength. Be my strength.* Sometimes the temptation is so great that you are not even able to formulate your own words in your head. It is then that you will learn the value of those simple prayers that the modern world despises so much: "Our Father, who art in heaven . . ." (Matthew 6:9) or "Hail Mary, full of grace . . . " (Luke 1:28).

Whatever you do, don't dialogue with the devil. He always has more questions than you have answers. He will suggest one thing and you will reply in thought with a rebuttal. This will go on, over and over again: He raises a thought and you reply. But the back-and-forth will wear you out. Eventually you will give in to the sin out of sheer exhaustion or just to end the dialogue. Sin is exhausting; avoid the dialogue that precedes it. Temptation is real; get to know how it takes place in your life, and avoid those people, places, and situations that create moments of temptation for you. When the tempter whispers in your ear, turn your back on him. Why complicate your life? Don't dialogue with the tempter. Turn to God and pray. You will be happier and you will have the peace of Christ in your heart.

To know your strengths and weaknesses is a great advantage in any field. In the spiritual realm it is of ultimate importance. The proud basketball player doesn't notice the faults in his game. The proud businesswoman doesn't notice the weaknesses in her leadership style. A proud artist doesn't notice the defect in her style. The proud man doesn't notice the weakness in his character.

The proud must content themselves with mediocrity; excellence belongs to the humble. Humble yourself to know who you really are and God will respond by revealing the incredible person you are capable of becoming.

• The Touch of the Master's Hand •

In her wisdom, my fourth-grade teacher, Mrs. Rutter, introduced my classmates and me to the following poem. After reciting it one day, she announced that over the next week, we were all to learn the poem by heart. Then every day for about a month someone would recite the poem for the class. It was just one example of her many moments of genius. At the time, our understanding of it was shallow, perhaps because one must experience some of life's hard knocks to truly appreciate the full meaning. The piece is titled "The Touch of the Master's Hand" and is by Myra B. Welch. Amazing things are possible if we allow the Master to lay his hands on our lives.

> 'Twas battered and scarred, and the auctioneer
> Thought it scarcely worth his while
> To waste much time on the old violin,
> But held it up with a smile.
> "What am I bidden, good folks," he cried,
> "Who'll start the bidding for me?"
> "A dollar, a dollar," then, two! Only two?
> "Two dollars, and who'll make it three?"
> "Three dollars, once; three dollars twice;
> Going for three . . ." But no,
> From the room, far back, a grey haired man
> Came forward and picked up the bow;
> Then, wiping the dust from the old violin,
> And tightening the loose strings,
> He played a melody pure and sweet
> As a caroling angel sings.
>
> The music ceased, and the auctioneer,
> With a voice that was quiet and low,
> Said, "What am I bid for the old violin?"
> And held it up with the bow.
> "A thousand dollars, and who'll make it two?
> Two thousand! And who'll make it three?
> Three thousand, once; three thousand twice;
> And going and gone," said he.
> The people cheered, but some of them cried,

"We do not quite understand
What changed its worth?" Swift came the reply:
"The touch of a master's hand."

And many a man with life out of tune,
And battered and scarred with sin,
Is auctioned cheap to the thoughtless crowd
Much like the old violin.
A "mess of potage," a glass of wine;
A game—and he travels on.
He is "going" once, and "going" twice,
He's "going" and almost "gone."
But the Master comes and the foolish crowd
Never can quite understand
The worth of a soul and the change that's wrought
By the touch of the Master's hand.

Chapter Two

DAILY PRAYER

Almost every day I meet people who tell me they are writing a book. Others tell me they have always wanted to write a book. I always encourage them, but in my heart I know that very few will actually ever write the book they tell me about. Most people like the idea of writing a book because it intrigues them. They get caught up in the idea of losing themselves in the creative process. But the reality is writing a book is just hard work. The beginning, when you conceive the idea for the book, is wonderful and exciting. But that doesn't last very long and then the hard work begins. Throughout the process there will be times when you catch a wave of inspiration, but if you wrote only when you felt inspired you would never finish your book.

Writing a book requires daily discipline. You have to work at it every day, even if some days all you do is read over what you wrote yesterday to keep it fresh in your mind. Writing a book requires the discipline to write when you feel like it *and* when you don't. Most people don't have this discipline, which is why many who start writing a book never finish it. When we think of writing a book we conjure romantic images of the artist at work in an inspirational setting, effortlessly penning page after page. The truth is, as already mentioned, writing a book is mostly hard work, and we are still just talking about writing a book. We have not spoken of writing a good book or even a great book yet.

Prayer is similar in many ways. Many people fail to establish a daily habit of prayer in their lives because they approach it with the wrong expectations. Consciously or subconsciously, most people approach prayer expecting it to be easy. The truth is, prayer is perhaps the most difficult thing we will ever do. From time to time, we may get carried away by a moment of inspiration in our prayer, but for the most part prayer is hard work—work well worth doing, but hard work nonetheless.

You don't become a great athlete by training only when you feel like it. You don't become a great writer by writing only when you feel inspired to write. And the saints did not become such fine ambassadors of God on earth by praying only when they felt like praying. In each case, a daily discipline is required.

Many years ago I saw a violinist interviewed. At the time he was considered the best in the world. He explained to the interviewer that he practiced for eight to ten hours each day. The interviewer implied that surely at this stage in his career he could ease up a little with the practice. The violinist smiled and said, "If I miss practice one day and perform the next night, I am the only person who can tell. But I can tell. My performance is off. If I missed practice every day for a week and then performed, there would only be a handful of people in any audience who would be able to tell that my performance was off. But if I missed practice for two weeks, or three weeks, almost every person in the audience would be able to tell that I was not performing at my best."

The same is true of prayer. If you neglect prayer for a day, you are probably the only person who can tell. But you can tell. You have less patience and you are less focused. If you neglect prayer for a week, several people around you will notice the change in you. But if you neglect prayer for two or three weeks, almost everyone around you will recognize that you are not at your best.

Prayer is central to the Christian experience. A Christian life is not sustainable without it, because growth in the Christian life is simply not possible without prayer. Growing in character and virtue, learning to hear the voice of God in our lives and walking where he calls us—all require the discipline of prayer. And it is not enough simply to pray when we feel like it. Prayer requires a daily commitment.

• Why Pray? •

A few months ago I was visiting a grade school, and a child, perhaps seven years old, asked me, "Why do you pray?" Sometimes a question is so simple and yet so striking that it causes you to pause time and time again to ponder the answer. This child's question was just such a question for me.

I know all the right answers to the questions. The catechism tells us that the purposes and forms of prayer are adoration, petition, intercession, thanksgiving, and praise. But I knew this answer would not satisfy my curious young friend.

Therese of Lisieux, one of the great teachers of Christian prayer, wrote, "For me, prayer is a surge of the heart; it is a simple look turned toward heaven, it is a cry of recognition and of love, embracing both trial and joy." But I am fairly sure if I had used that as my answer, the seven-year-old student would have just looked at me with a blank stare.

Dozens of thoughts and answers flashed through my mind, all of which may have suited an adult or a theologian, but I couldn't find the words to express them to a child. So, I asked him a question instead of answering his. I asked him the same question he had asked me: "Why do you pray?"

He didn't have to think about it. Spontaneously and casually he said, "Well, God is my friend, and friends like to know what is going on in each other's lives."

Sometimes I pray for very selfish reasons. Perhaps I am stressed and overwhelmed, and I go to prayer hoping God will calm my heart and mind and bring peace to my soul. Sometimes I pray for completely altruistic reasons. When some region of the world is torn apart by natural disaster or war, I often find myself driven to prayer. And sometimes I pray for very holy reasons. There are times when I pray not because I want something from God, but just to express my gratitude for all the things, people, and opportunities he has filled my life with. And when I am at my best, I pray simply to be with God and seek his ways.

Most of the time I pray for more practical reasons—three in particular. First, I pray to make sense of things. Life is often complex and confusing, but in the midst of all that, God always seems to present a simple path. The ways of the Lord may not be easy, and at times may be tremendously difficult, but they are almost always simple.

I also pray because I want to live life deeply and deliberately. I am not confused about how precious a gift life is, and I want to fully experience that gift. In high school these words of Thoreau became engraved on my heart: "I went to the woods because I wanted to live deliberately, I wanted to live deep and suck out all the marrow of life, to put to rout all that is not life and not when I had come to die discover that I had not lived." I go to the woods of prayer each day for the same reason.

The third of the very practical reasons I pray is to build up the kind of inner density required to prevent the culture from swallowing me up.

We live in a time of tremendous cultural pressure. The spirit of the world is powerful and unrelenting, and there is little societal support for those who choose to reject the spirit of the world and embrace the Spirit of God. This is not a popular choice, and as a result, it can often lead to a certain loneliness in our lives.

Osmosis is the scientific theory that essentially states that what is more dense will filter through to what is less dense. If we are going to be true to our values, if we are going to celebrate and defend the-best-version-of-ourselves, we need to build up a certain density within us. This inner strength, or density, will allow us to resist the cultural pressure to abandon our values, our true selves, and God.

If we are going to walk with God and become the-best-version-of-ourselves, we need this inner density, which seems to be created by a combination of grace and discipline. This inner density is not something we can attain for ourselves; it is a gift God freely gives us when we cooperate with his plan for our lives. When we have this density within us, we will have a Christian effect on our environment. When we don't have this density, our environment has an effect on us. What is more dense filters through to what is less dense, and the cultural density all around us is intense. The most powerful way to build this density, this inner strength, is through prayer and the sacraments. I pray to gather density to survive and thrive in a culture that is often hostile and sometimes violent toward what is good and true and noble.

It is almost twenty years now since I began a serious habit of prayer in my life. Now I cannot imagine a life without prayer. I don't know how people survive in our crazy, noisy, busy world without the sanctuary of prayer to renew and refresh them. There are many reasons to pray and many ways to pray—what is critical is that we make an effort to create a daily habit of prayer in our lives.

• Thought Determines Action •

To contemplate is to ponder something deeply. As Christians we are called to think on a deeper level, and to live on a deeper level. Daily prayer makes this possible. It is in our prayer that we move beyond the fleeting thoughts of life and begin to lead meaningful lives of contemplation.

Contemplation is not just for monks and nuns. In truth, we all lead lives of contemplation, but we spend our lives contemplating very different things. What do *you* contemplate? Is it the riches of the world? Is it every woman who passes you in the street? Do you ponder the latest fashions? The local gossip? Or do you contemplate the wonders of God, the glory of his creation, and the joys of the spiritual life?

It is not necessary to go away to a monastery to live a life of contemplation. We are all contemplatives because we are all thinking all the time, and what you contemplate will play a very significant role in the life you live.

The reason prayer and contemplation are so integral to the Christian life is because thought determines action. If you send your thoughts down one road, your actions will follow your thoughts. Thought determines action, and so the actions of your life are determined by your most dominant thoughts.

For a moment, imagine you are a basketball player. It's game seven in the NBA playoffs. There is one second left on the clock. The scores are tied. You have just been fouled, and you have one shot from the free throw line.

Between the moment the foul is called and the time you shoot the ball, everything moves in slow motion. There are millions of people watching you, but really there is just you and your thoughts. During those moments before shooting, if you imagine yourself missing the shot, you will miss the shot. If you imagine yourself making the shot, you will make the shot. But what if, in that brief time, you have forty-seven thoughts of missing the shot and only thirteen thoughts of making the shot? What will happen then? You'll miss it. Why? Because the actions of your life are determined by your most *dominant* thought.

Consider the heroes of Christianity, the men and women we call saints. They have lived in every place, in every time, and in every culture. Some of the saints were young and some were old. Some were rich and some were poor. Some were educated and others were uneducated. Some had positions of power and authority and others did not. My point is that you cannot find a more diverse group of people in history than the saints. And yet, the people of their time say exactly the same thing about every single one of them: They brought Jesus to life fo us. What did they say about Francis of Assisi? He brought Jesus to life for us. They said the same about Therese of Lisieux, Ignatius of Loyola, Catherine of Siena, and Dominic. What did they say about Mother Teresa and John Paul II? They brought Jesus to life for us in our own place and time.

For two thousand years men and women have been saying exactly the same thing about each and every one of the saints. Why? Because the saints all spent their post-conversion lives pondering the life and teachings of Jesus Christ—the Gospel—and they simply became what they thought. Human thought is creative. What we think becomes.

Some of the saints were converted from other faiths and others were converted from incredibly wayward lives, but most of them were converted from a very common complacency toward God's will for their lives. Are you ready to begin your post-conversion life?

When I was in middle school, we went away on retreat. At that time, I was more or less disinterested in things of a spiritual nature, yet I seem to remember vaguely that the theme of the retreat was placing Christ at the center of our lives. For three days every speaker shared about living a "Christ-centered" life.

Since that time, I have discovered that this is not just a nice phrase or idea, but that it is, in fact, the very core of our Catholic spirituality. The centrality of Christ in human history and in our individual lives is no small discovery, nor is it just an idea. It is an idea that has been tried and tested, and the results are awe-inspiring.

But if I am honest with myself, despite my deep desire, it is a constant struggle to keep Christ at the center of my life. There are moments when there is no question he is at the center of my life. Sometimes there are days at a time when I am able to place God and his will at the center of my life, but then I get distracted by the many conflicting desires of my heart and all the things of this world that lure me away from God and the-best-version-of-myself.

My thoughts always wander before my actions do. Thought determines action, and before too long, you will be living out what has already happened in your mind. Human thought is creative. What we think becomes. What you allow to occupy your mind forms the reality of your life. Good or bad, almost everything happens in your mind before it happens in time and space. There are accidents and things beyond our control, certainly. In these cases we can only control how we respond to such unexpected circumstances. If you can direct what happens in your mind, you can massively influence what happens in your life, and completely direct how you respond to what happens in your life.

So, what are you thinking? What do you think about all day long? What do you think about in the car on the way to and from work each day? What do you think about while you are waiting in line at the supermarket?

Whatever you place your mental attention on will increase in your life. If you place your attention on money, you will have more money. If you place your attention on how much you are loved (or not loved), you will have more love (or not) in your life. If you place your attention on virtue, you will have more virtue. And if you place your mental attention on the life and teachings of Jesus Christ, he will increase in you (cf. John 3:30).

Paul gives us this advice: "Whatever is true, whatever is honorable, whatever is just, whatever is pure, whatever is lovely, whatever is gracious, if there is any excellence, if there is anything worthy of praise, think about these things." (Philippians 4:8) And to my mind while Paul could have been speaking about many things of this world and the next, his description of what we should think about is at the same time a description of the Gospel and an invitation to ponder Christ and his teachings.

Earlier we said that the difference between the saints and those who have been less successful in living the Christian life was that the saints affixed their singleness of purpose on doing the will of God and that they had better habits. These habits were not only external habits but also internal habits. One of those critical internal habits was the habit of the mind we call contemplation. Too often we just let our thoughts wander. God invites us to focus our thoughts, and the discipline of daily prayer teaches us how to direct those thoughts toward the higher things.

As you move from one activity to the next in your day, become aware of what you are thinking and how different thoughts make you feel. Become aware of the thoughts that encourage you to love God and those around you more, and those thoughts that don't. Then consciously try to focus more and more of your thinking on those that do. When you realize that your mind is wandering toward negative, self-destructive, or gossip-ridden thoughts, steer your mind in another direction.

You cannot grow an oak tree with an apple seed. You cannot grow a good life with bad thoughts. Certain thoughts give birth to certain actions. With each passing day God invites you to change, to grow, and to become a-better-version-of-yourself. God loves you as you are, but he loves you too much to let you stay that way.

• The Classroom of Silence •

If I asked you to conduct a search for some suitable candidates to be leaders and prophets in the modern world, where would you look? You probably wouldn't immediately start looking for shepherds. I have always found it interesting that the most common profession among the prophets and leaders of the Old Testament was shepherding. Why do you suppose God called so many shepherds to occupy positions of authority and influence? What made them uniquely suited?

It seems to me these shepherds spent long hours in silence and solitude. They were immersed day after day in God's cosmic temple. This produced in them a unique understanding of nature and creation, making them worthy stewards of the earth and all that is in it. But these long days spent immersed in the classroom of silence also provided them with plenty of time to think, reflect, and contemplate. And most importantly, this silence and solitude gave them more opportunity than most to hear and listen to the voice of God in their lives.

When we read the Bible it seems the most common preface to any sentence is "God said." "God said to Adam . . . ," "God said to Noah . . . ," "God said to Abraham . . . ," "God said to Moses . . . ," and on and on. Throughout the history of God's relationship with humanity he has constantly been communicating with us. I am convinced that in this modern time it is not that God has stopped speaking to us, but rather that we have stopped listening. And while I believe that God can communicate through anyone and anything at any time, his preferred venue is still silence and solitude. In the silence God speaks. Or perhaps it is just that in the silence, away from the hustle and bustle of the world, we are able to hear him.

If I live to be a hundred and write for my whole life, I will never be able to emphasize enough how important silence is as an ingredient of the spiritual life. In *A Call to Joy* I wrote, "You can learn more in an hour of silence than you can in a year from books." In *Mustard Seeds* I wrote, "It is in the classroom of silence that God bestows his wisdom on men and women."

I will make two promises to you: In the silence you will find God and in the silence you will find yourself. These will be the two greatest discoveries of your life. But these discoveries will not be moments of epiphany; they will be gradual. You will discover a little at a time, something like a jigsaw puzzle being put together. I cannot imagine how miserable life would be without the adventure of discovering God and self. It is this process of discovery that allows us to make sense of life.

In the silence things start to make sense. Consider this example: You are taking a road trip and you get lost or a little turned around. What do you do? Do you tell the people you are traveling with to talk louder and turn the music up? No. You ask everyone to be quiet and you turn the music off. Why? Things start to make sense in the silence.

Now, applying this to our personal lives, we are all trying to make sense of something in our lives right now. We are all constantly trying to make sense of something in our lives. You are trying right now. What is that something? Are you giving yourself the silence you need to make sense of it?

Our modern world is spinning out of control, and one of the chief contributors to the chaos and confusion of our modern age is noise. Our lives are filled with noise. We are afraid of silence.

During the 1940s, C. S. Lewis wrote a series of letters that appeared in a London newspaper called *The Guardian*. These letters were the humorous and insightful correspondence between a senior devil, Screwtape, and an apprentice devil, his nephew Wormwood. The thirty-one letters were later published in the form of a book titled *The Screwtape Letters*. In the letters, Screwtape is advising Wormwood about the procedure for winning a soul away from God for the devil. At one point, Wormwood is trying to think up all kinds of exotic ways to tempt the man who has been assigned to him, and Screwtape rebukes him, explaining that their methods have long been established. One such method, he explains, is to create so much noise that men and women can no longer hear the voice of God in their lives. In one letter, the senior devil Screwtape announces, "We will make the whole universe a noise in the end." Can you hear the voice of God in your life?

I believe the writings of C. S. Lewis were operating in a prophetic capacity when he expressed this idea more than sixty years ago. Today, we wake up to clock radios, we listen to the radio while we shower, and we watch television while we eat breakfast. We listen to the radio in the car on the way to work or school, we listen to music all day over the intercom, we get put on hold and we listen to music. We have Game Boys, pagers, cell phones, Walkmans, Discmans, portable DVD players, iPods, and iPhones. Most homes have multiple televisions, and we leave them on even when nobody is watching them. We have so much noise we can't even hear ourselves think.

How do you imagine that in the midst of all that noise you are going to work out who you are and what you are here for? The reality is, you won't. Unless you withdraw from all the noise of your life and the world for a few minutes each day, you will most likely just become another cog in the global economic wheel, consuming and being consumed.

Our world has been filled with noise, and as a result, we can no longer hear the voice of God in our lives. It is time to enter into the classroom of silence.

• Getting Started •

This is how my commitment to daily prayer began. At the time I was in high school. Everything at school was going very well—I had a great group of friends, a wonderful girlfriend, and a good part-time job. On the outside everything seemed fine, but on the inside a growing restlessness was building up.

My heart was restless. I sensed something was missing in my life. I knew something was wrong, but I couldn't pinpoint it. I sensed there must be more to life, but I didn't know what it was, or where to find it. I tried to ignore these feelings, but the nagging restlessness persisted.

Several weeks later I bumped into a family friend and he asked me how school was going. "Fine," I replied. He is a doctor, so he knows how to ask the right questions, and for five or ten minutes he gently probed the different areas of my life. Each question and each answer led us a little closer to his diagnosis. Then he paused briefly, looked deep into my eyes, and said, "You're not really happy, are you, Matthew?"

He knew it and I knew it, but I was ashamed to admit it at first. But our lives seem to flood with grace at unexpected moments, and I began to tell him about the emptiness and restlessness I was experiencing. After listening to me carefully he suggested I stop by my church for ten minutes each morning on the way to school.

I listened, smiled, nodded politely, and immediately dismissed him as some sort of religious fanatic. As he expanded on his idea and how it would transform my life, I wondered to myself, *How is ten minutes of prayer each day going to help me?* Before he had finished speaking I had resolved to completely ignore everything he said.

In the coming weeks I threw myself into my studies, my work, and my sporting pursuits with more vigor than ever before. I had done this to appease my restless heart at other times in my life. But achievement in these areas no longer brought the fulfillment it once had.

One morning about six weeks later the emptiness had become so great that I found myself stopping by church on the way to school. I crept quietly into the church, sat near the back, and began to plan my day. Just planning the day ahead of me lifted the clouds of hurried confusion. For the first time in my life I tasted a few drops of that wonderful tonic we call peace—and I liked it.

The next day, and every day, I returned. Each morning I would simply sit toward the back of the church and move through the events of the day in my mind. With each passing day a sense of peace, purpose, and direction began to fill me.

Then one day as I sat there it occurred to me that "planning my day" wasn't really prayer. So I began to pray: *God, I want this . . . and I need this . . . and could you do this for me . . . and help me with this . . . and let this happen . . . and please, don't let that happen. . . .*

For the next few weeks, this is how it went. Every morning I would stop by church, sit toward the back, plan my day, and tell God what I wanted. For a while this was the depth of my prayer life. And then one day I had a problem. That morning I came to the church and with a simple prayer in my heart, I looked up toward the tabernacle and began to explain, *God, I've got this problem. . . . This is the situation. . . . These are the circumstances. . . .*

Then I stumbled onto the question that would change my life forever: *God, what do you think I should do?*

With that question my life began to change. Asking that question marked a new beginning in my life. Up until then, I had only ever prayed, *Listen up, God, your servant is speaking.* But in that moment of spontaneous prayer the Spirit that guides us all led me to pray, *Speak, Lord, your servant is listening.* It was perhaps the first moment of honest and humble prayer in my life. Before that day, I had only been interested in telling God what *my* will was. Now for the first time I was asking God to reveal his will.

God, what do you think I should do? I call this the Big Question. It is the question that changed my life forever, and the question that continues to transform my life on a daily basis when I have the courage to ask it.

This question should be a constant theme in our spiritual lives. When we are attentive to it we are happy regardless of external realities, because we have a peace and contentment within. It is the peace that comes from knowing that who we are and what we are doing makes sense regardless of the outcome, and regardless of other people's opinions. This peace comes from taking into account the only opinion that truly matters: God's.

Every day you make dozens of decisions, some of them large and some of them small. When was the last time you invited God into the decisions of your life?

I *try* each day to let God play a role in my decision making, but often the allure of this world distracts me. Sometimes I simply forget to consult him. Sometimes I block his voice out because I want to do something I know he doesn't want me to do. Sometimes I foolishly believe that I know a shortcut to happiness. These decisions always lead me to misery of one form or another.

There is only one question and one course of action that leads to lasting happiness in this changing world: *God, what do you think I should do?* To think that we can find happiness without asking this question is one of the grandest delusions.

Ignatius asked the question. Francis asked the question. Benedict asked the question. Dominic asked the question. Joan of Arc asked the question. Theresa asked the question. But will you? We need saints today. These men and women began by asking a very simple question: *God, what do you think I should do?* And as a result of constantly asking this question they became giants of their age. Our age needs its own spiritual giants.

Sometimes when we talk about the saints we make the mistake of thinking that they were different from us. They were not. To be a saint is to decide for God and with God. You and I make decisions every day. Some of them are large but most of them are small. But when was the last time you sat down with the Divine Architect and asked, *God, what do you think I should do in this situation with my spouse?* When was the last time you sat down with the Divine Navigator and asked, *God, what do you think I should do in this situation at work?* When your kids come to you to talk about what they are thinking of doing with their lives, do you just ask them what they want to do? Or do you ask them what they feel God is calling them to?

I've known happy people and I've known miserable people, and I can tell you without any shadow of a doubt that the difference between the truly happy people in this world and the miserable people is one thing: a sense of mission.

People who are passionate, energetic, and enthusiastic about life have a sense of mission in their lives. They are not living their lives in the selfish pursuit of pleasure or possessions. They are living out a mission, and through that mission, they are making a difference in other people's lives.

What's your mission? How will you discover your mission? Perhaps the first realization is you don't choose a mission—you get sent on a mission.

"Most men lead lives of quiet desperation." If you don't ask the big question, you won't discover your mission, and sooner or later you will be numbered among Thoreau's masses. You won't plan to live a life of quiet desperation; nobody does. You'll just wake up one morning and wonder how you got there.

If you are already living a life of quiet desperation, you don't have to stay there. Just start asking the big question. *God, what do you think I should do?* In the moments of the day ask the question. In your daily prayer, ask the question. Make this one question a constant part of your inner dialogue, and I promise you, your life will start to change.

Life is vocational, meaning it is about seeking, finding, and living out your mission, your vocation. We talk a lot about vocation, but I don't get the sense that the average person really knows what it means. With the current shortage of vocations to the priesthood, our discussions about vocations tend to be focused on priesthood. We acknowledge that marriage, religious life, and the single life are also vocations, but our discussion, education, and prayer for vocations seem to be focused almost exclusively on our need for priests. All this leaves many people thinking that some have a vocation and others don't.

The idea of vocation in general has nothing to do with priesthood. Vocation is about finding what you are best suited to. It's about finding your mission in life, discovering who God has created you to be and what tasks he has created you to carry out in this world. Everyone has a vocation, and finding it truly is the single event that will create more happiness in our lives than anything else. Life, therefore, is about vocation. It is about seeking and finding what God has created you for—and then doing it. It is through this process that God will transform you into the-best-version-of-yourself and the world into the place he intended it to be.

Some people are best suited to marriage, some are best suited to priesthood, some to religious life, and others to being single. These are the vocations we tend to speak of, but everyone is different. Some priests work in parishes and others in universities. There are a thousand ways to live out the vocation to priesthood. The same is true for marriage, religious life, and the single life.

Each of us is created for a reason. The important thing to remember is that *you* have a vocation. Everyone has a vocation, and unveiling it is critically important to our experience of life, because life is vocational. For this reason, when we speak, teach, or pray about vocations we should personalize it for each individual. Vocation is deeply personal.

Every single one of us has an overwhelming desire for happiness and the different ways we respond to this desire. In the end, it seems it all comes down to deciding how long you want to be happy. If you are willing to trade happiness for moments of pleasure, I suspect sex, drugs, food, alcohol, and gambling will be your things. But I want more than that. How long do you want to be happy for? If you just want to be happy for an hour, take a nap. If you want to be happy for a whole day, go shopping. If you want to be happy for a weekend, go fishing. If you want to be happy for a month, take a vacation to Australia. If you want to be happy for a whole year, inherit a fortune. If you want to be happy for a decade, find a way to make a difference in other people's lives. But if you want to be happy for a lifetime and beyond, seek the will of God for your life. Don't overwhelm yourself. Seek it one day at a time, one moment at a time, one decision at a time.

Several months after I first began visiting our local church for ten minutes each morning, a very wise old man said to me, "You are unhappy. Think to yourself: 'There must be an obstacle between God and me.' You will seldom be wrong."

Years later I was on a plane just about every day and I got into the habit of writing one small passage each day. I would then use these passages to guide my thoughts, actions, and reflections for that day. A collection of those passages was later published as *Mustard Seeds*. This is one of my favorites: "When you know you are doing the will of God, that alone is enough to sustain your happiness. When you don't have that, all the possessions in the world cannot sustain happiness in the depths of your heart."

The will of God is a mysterious thing. In my own spiritual journey I have learned that God reveals His will one step at a time. This creates a great deal of uncertainty, and we don't like that. We want to know where we are going and when we will get there. In this modern age we try to control all the elements so that we can have security and stability. If only we could learn to enjoy uncertainty. Uncertainty is a sign that all is well. God is your friend; he will take care of the details.

Our lives change when our habits change. My life changed when, encouraged by a friend, I began to pray for ten minutes a day. In those quiet moments of reflection I stumbled upon the big question: *God, what do you think I should do?*

For many years I have been traveling around the world speaking to different groups of people. I cannot remember a time when I have not urged my listeners to enter into the classroom of silence for ten minutes of prayer and reflection each day. As these years have passed, millions of people have attended my talks, seminars, and retreats, and sometimes I cannot help but wonder how many of those have actually formed the habit of spending ten minutes in prayer each day. Often people dismiss the message as too simple. It is the simple things that have a tremendous ability to transform our lives. I have experienced the power of simplicity in my own life and I invite you to do the same.

So now it is your turn. Before you go to bed tonight, take a small piece of paper and write these four words on it: TEN MINUTES A DAY. Stick that piece of paper on the mirror in your bathroom where you brush your teeth. Tomorrow morning when you are brushing your teeth decide a time during your day when you will spend ten minutes in the classroom of silence with your God in prayer. If at all possible, stop by your church. It is probably empty and quiet for most of the day. I know we can pray anywhere, but there is something mystical and powerful about God's presence at Church.

I challenge you to make daily prayer a priority in your life, and to make it an indispensable part of your daily schedule. Enter into the classroom of silence. Sit with the Divine Architect and together design something wonderful. Visit with the Divine Navigator and plot a course to uncharted territories. Sit with God and dream some dreams.

Ten minutes a day. If you are confused, angry, tired, frustrated, happy, excited, grateful . . . come to the silence. Stick a note on your bathroom mirror. TEN MINUTES A DAY. And every day as you brush your teeth, ask yourself, "When will I spend my ten minutes in the classroom of silence today?" Don't be deceived by the simplicity of this message. You will be amazed how much ten minutes each day in a quiet church can change your life.

In time you may decide to spend more than ten minutes each day, and that is wonderful. There may be days when you are able to sit with God for an hour or two, and it is wonderful to have this carefree timelessness with him from time to time. But regardless of how busy you are, defend and celebrate your ten minutes every day.

It would be nice if our souls growled when they were hungry, like our stomachs do. But they don't. Your immortal soul is the most valuable possession you have—feed it, nurture it, celebrate it. The saints realized the value of their immortal souls, so they made it a priority to nourish and nurture them. I hope one day soon you will realize this too, not only in your mind, but in your heart and deep within your being. And I hope that, having come to this realization, you will begin to nourish and nurture your soul. Only then will you truly thrive.

Ten minutes a day. Begin today. The beginning of anything is the most difficult; getting started is the tough part. Recognize it so that you don't get discouraged. The space shuttle uses ninety-six percent of its fuel at takeoff, but then it virtually glides through space and back to earth. Get started.

• Do I Have to Go to Church to Pray? •

I hope in these past few pages I have convinced you to begin (or renew) the discipline of daily prayer—not just when you feel like it, or when it is convenient, but every day. The next question for us to consider is where you should pray.

Whenever I tell people the story of how I started spending ten minutes a day at church, I get the question, "Do I have to go to church to pray?" The short answer is no. You can pray anywhere, and spontaneous prayer should be something that accompanies you wherever you go. We can pray while we are driving to work and while we are exercising, while we are doing the shopping or washing the dishes, the moment we learn that a friend is sick or as a speeding ambulance passes us on the road. Prayer should spring forth from the daily events of our lives. But we also need a time of focused prayer each day, a time set aside from everything else, when we give our undivided attention to God. Does this time have to be spent at church? The short answer is no. But allow me to pose another question: Where is the best place to spend your daily prayer time?

There are many days when I don't pray at church, but I always yearn to. When I am able to get to a church for my daily prayer time, my prayer seems more focused and fruitful. I have thought long and hard about why this is and I have reached two conclusions. One is a very natural reason. The other is the most astonishing spiritual reality our faith has to offer.

The first is that our churches are quiet and designed for prayer. They lend themselves easily to the spiritual, and provide a place set apart. In the Scriptures we read over and over again about Jesus going alone to a quiet place. He would go to a place set apart from everyone and everything else so that he could pray. If Jesus needed to do this, I know how much more I need it.

The second reason I think my daily prayer time seems more effective when I am able to spend that time in a church is the supernatural reason. I believe that Jesus Christ is present in the Eucharist, and that he is present in a very unique and powerful way in every tabernacle, in every Catholic church around the world. I think his presence makes a difference. How could it not?

There are many people who do not believe that Jesus is present in the Eucharist. In John's Gospel Jesus says, "I am the living bread . . . whoever eats this bread shall live forever," (John 6:51) "Unless you eat my flesh and drink my blood you do not have life within you," (John 6:53) "Whoever eats my flesh and drinks my blood remains in me and I in him." (John 6:56) Many of Jesus' followers at the time left him because of these statements, just as many of Jesus' followers today have left his Church because of our belief that he is present in the Eucharist. In the Gospel after Jesus speaks of this we read, "This saying is hard, who can accept it?" and "As a result many of his disciples returned to their former way of life and no longer accompanied him." (John 6:66)

I can understand how those who don't believe in the true presence of Christ in the Eucharist would discount the power of praying at church. But once you believe that Jesus is present, how could you believe that the presence of the Eucharist would not make a difference?

Years ago, I received a letter from a priest who had worked as a lay missionary in China before he returned to his homeland of America and became a priest. He shared many stories about the Church in China, but there is one that made a huge impression on me. It is a story I have told hundreds of times and one that always humbles me.

Many years after being ordained a priest, he returned to China, incognito, for a brief visit. Even today, there are priests and bishops in prison in China for nothing other than refusing to let the Communist government control their churches. For this reason, nobody in China knew that he was a priest.

On the second night of his visit, he was awakened in the middle of the night by the noise of people moving around the house. A little scared, he got up and went to his door. Opening it, he asked one of the men living in the house what was going on.

His Chinese host replied, "We're going to the wall."

He inquired further, "What is the wall?"

His host replied, "Come with us and we will show you."

There were more than twenty people living in the small house, and while none of them knew he was a priest, they knew he could be trusted.

Not satisfied with the answers he had received, he went downstairs and found one of the older women whom he had known many, many years earlier and asked her, "What's going on? Where are you all going?"

She gently replied, "We're going to the wall."

He persisted, "Yes, but what is the wall?"

She replied with the same gentleness, "Come with us and we will show you."

He got dressed and ventured out into the night with the group. They walked for miles and along the way other groups joined them. Now, all together, they numbered almost 120 men, women, and children. Soon they came to a forest and as they began to walk into it, he noticed that some of the men in the group were climbing trees.

Several minutes later they came to a clearing in the forest, and in the middle of the clearing was a small wall about four feet tall, from an old, derelict building. The old woman turned to him and smiled with all the love in her heart, and though he sensed an incredible excitement in her he did not know what to make of it. The people seemed excited, but he was scared.

Looking up into the trees, he noticed that there was a circle of men in the trees surrounding the clearing. And now, as the group came close to the wall, they fell down on their knees before it.

Moments later, one man got up and walked toward the wall, then, reaching out with one hand, he took a single brick out of the wall. Behind the brick was a tiny monstrance holding the Eucharist. The group spent one hour in silent prayer before the Blessed Sacrament, and then the same man got up, approached the wall, and replaced the single brick. The men came down from their lookout positions in the trees and the group went quietly home.

The next day he told the people that he was a priest and they told him that they had not had Mass in their village for ten years. Once or twice a week they would go to the wall in the middle of the night, risking their lives, to spend an hour with Jesus, truly present in the Eucharist.

The following night, the priest said Mass at the wall and replaced the host. It was one of the highlights of his priesthood.

I am not sure we appreciate the power of God present among us in every tabernacle in every Church. If this priest had been discovered that night he would have been imprisoned and tortured, and the rest of the group would have been imprisoned and quite possibly executed. They knew this all too well, and it was a risk they were willing to take.

There is something very powerful about spending time in a quiet church. I would like to invite you to explore this experience. Over the years, I have visited many churches, but there are a few that I go back to time and time again. When I was growing up in Sydney, my family and I belonged to St. Martha's Parish, and it is there that I first started spending my ten minutes each day in prayer. I always look forward to spending time there when I am back in Sydney visiting my family and friends. Below the tabernacle it reads, "My Lord and My God," and this simple phrase had a profound effect on me. These days, when I am at home in Cincinnati, I like to spend my prayer time in the chapel at a Franciscan monastery not too far from my home. The friars have a series of chairs gathered around the tabernacle, and I like to sit there close to it and talk to Jesus about what is happening in my life.

Experience has taught me time and time again that all the answers are in the tabernacle. I can go to many people in my life and ask them what they think I should do in a given situation, but nothing compares to sitting before Jesus in the tabernacle and placing my question before him.

Beyond the power of silence in the lives of individuals and the power of Christ's presence in our tabernacles, I can attest also to the power of silence and his presence in a community. There is a phenomenon reemerging in the Catholic world known as Eucharistic adoration. There are more and more parishes that have adoration chapels, and many of them are open twenty-four hours a day. It may be considered old-fashioned and overly pious by some, but my experience has been that wherever you find Eucharistic adoration in a parish, those communities are more vibrant. The people are more spiritually focused, more involved, more generous with God, and the communities tend to be thriving.

When are we finally going to stop casting these signs aside as if they were merely coincidence? It seems that adoration chapels draw people closer to God, deeper into the spiritual life, and provide something people desperately need at this time.

It can be very hard to find a quiet place in this world. But this quietness is essential to the growth in the Spirit. Your soul needs silence like you need air to breathe and water to drink. I pray that as the noise of the world becomes louder and more constant we will continue to dedicate ourselves to providing places set apart for people to experience God in the silence they so desperately need.

While modern man is filling his life with more and more noise and trying to absent God from more and more areas of his life, God is inviting us into the silence and into his presence. Here, in the presence of God, we will find rest for our weary hearts and minds. In the great classroom of silence we will develop resolute hearts and peaceful spirits. If you listen, you will hear Jesus speaking to you with a clarity that is unmistakable: "Come to me all you who labor and are heavy laden, and I will give you rest." (Matthew 11:28)

So, returning to the question at hand, do you have to pray at church? No, but if you are able, why wouldn't you? I realize that for some it is impossible. They are homebound or live in rural areas where the nearest church is fifty miles away. But for most of us it is simply a matter of making it a priority. Is it convenient? Probably not. But I don't think you and I do anything more important on any day than spending a few minutes with our God. Our daily commitment to prayer deserves to take priority in our lives, but too often we find ourselves caught up in all the urgent things. The problem with that is that the most important things are hardly ever urgent. Prayer allows us to work out what matters most and place it at the center of our lives.

All I ask of you is this: If at all possible, try what I describe here. Stop by your church for ten minutes each day for the next couple of weeks. If you can, do it first thing in the morning. I think you will find that your days are more fruitful and focused, and that you are filled with a passion that is invigorating and a joy that is intoxicating.

Come into the silence.

• Begin Today •

Perhaps your last concern is that you don't know how to pray. It is much simpler than you suppose. Step into the silence, and in your heart, say to God, *I don't know how to pray,* and already you will have begun to pray. Just talk to him. Simply open your heart to him in a gentle dialogue. Speak to him as you would a great friend, mentor, coach, or teacher.

When you leave your time of prayer, continue the dialogue with God in your heart throughout the moments of your day. Share with him your joys and your disappointments, your questions and your doubts. Speak to him about everything.

Tevye, from *Fiddler on the Roof,* is a great example. He is always talking to God, about everything. This constant dialogue is perhaps part of what

Paul had in mind when he wrote, "Pray constantly." (1 Thessalonians 5:17)

So, begin today with ten minutes. In time you may feel called to spend more time. If that is the case, I encourage you to increase the time you spend in prayer gradually and consistently. If it is going to be ten minutes a day, make it ten minutes a day—not six and not fourteen.

I would also like to encourage you to keep track of what days you do it, what days you don't, and how long you spend in prayer each day. In my work as a business consultant I have had the privilege of working with many Fortune 500 companies. One of the greatest lessons I have learned from the very best companies is that they measure everything. They have a fundamental understanding that if you don't measure it you won't change it. This lesson has led me to conclude that we measure very little in our lives the way the best companies measure everything in their business.

As a result I started measuring several things in my life. I started measuring how much time I spent in prayer each day, how much time I spent exercising each day, and what I ate each day. I wrote all of this down on a piece of paper throughout the day and at the end of each week I tallied it up. I was amazed how much I ate and how little I exercised. I was also surprised to see how little time I spent in prayer.

So I would like to encourage you to measure how much time you spend in prayer each week. Visit DynamicCatholic.com to download a card that you can print and carry with you as an easy way to keep track of the time you spend in prayer each week. You will be amazed how measuring this time allows you to focus and grow in your prayer life. You may also want to visit the site to discover what happened when a whole parish did this.

• Cast into the Deep •

When my soul is hungry I often think of the passage in Luke's Gospel. Simon and his friends have been fishing all night without catching anything. Jesus says to him, "Put out into the deep water and lower your nets for a catch." (Luke 5:4) You can imagine what Simon is thinking to himself. He has been fishing all night and this is his profession and he has caught nothing, and now Jesus, who has no knowledge or experience of fishing, is telling him to get back out there and lower his nets. If they were fishing all night you can be sure they are tired. If they caught nothing you can be sure they are frustrated. And it is important to note that putting out into the deep water and lowering the nets is not a five- or ten-minute exercise. Jesus is making a significant request.

Perhaps at this time in your life you are tired and frustrated—with your career, with your marriage, with your children, with society, with your spiritual life—but Jesus is saying to you, "Put out into the deep water and lower your nets for a catch."

In the story we know that Simon and his friends listen to Jesus and do what he suggests, and they catch so many fish that their nets begin to tear and they need help from fishermen in other boats to haul in the catch.

Over and over in life, God challenges us to abandon our doubts and fears and cast our nets into the deep waters of the spiritual life. It is never convenient, it is almost always difficult, and it is sometimes quite painful, but if we heed the Lord's direction we will always bring in a huge catch. Don't be afraid of the deep places.

As I have written this chapter my mind has time and time again been drawn back to a story that highlights the power and the purpose of daily prayer:

Once upon a time on a glorious summer's evening, in an ancient English castle in the hills on the outskirts of London, there was a banquet.

More than six hundred guests had traveled from all over the world to attend this lavish affair. There were movie stars and musicians, artists and politicians, princes and princesses, fashion designers and beautiful models, men and women who owned businesses large enough to be small countries, and a handful of others, of no particular note, who had endeared themselves to the host over the years.

The evening was to be celebrated not with music, or speeches, or dancing, but with a presentation by a famous Shakespearean actor.

The castle was radiant, adorned with a springtime of flowers and perfectly lit with a myriad of candles. The people enjoyed a sumptuous meal and a wonderful selection of the finest wines the world had to offer.

When the guests had finished their dinner, but before dessert was served, the host stood up and welcomed them. He then explained, "This evening, instead of music, and speeches, and dancing, I have invited England's most celebrated Shakespearean actor to perform for us." The people graciously applauded, and the actor stood, moved toward the center of the banquet hall, and began to speak.

He spoke eloquently and powerfully. For thirty-five minutes he moved about the banquet hall, brilliantly reciting famous passages from the writings of William Shakespeare.

"Oh, I am but fortune's fool . . ."

"To be or not to be—that is the question:
Whether 'tis nobler in the mind to suffer
The slings and arrows of outrageous fortune
Or to take arms against a sea of troubles . . ."
"Shall I compare thee to a summer's day?
Thou art more beautiful and more temperate . . ."

"Neither a borrower nor a lender be,
for loan oft loses both itself and a friend.
And borrowing dulleth the edge of husbandry.
This above all, to thine own self be true,
And it must follow as night follows day
Thou canst not then be false to any man."

After each brief episode the audience erupted in applause, and their applause echoed up through the castle and spilled out into the moonlit courtyards.

"'Tis but thy name that is my enemy: Thou art thyself . . . What's in a name? That which we call a rose by any other name would

smell as sweet;
So Romeo would, were he not Romeo call'd,
Retain thy dear perfection which he owes . . ."

"If we shadows have offended,
Think but this and all is mended,
That you have but slumbered here
While these visions did appear . . ."

With this, the closing passage from *A Midsummer Night's Dream,* the actor took a bow and announced that he was finished. The guests clapped and cheered and called for an encore. The actor rose to his feet once more to oblige his eager audience. "If anyone has a favorite Shakespearean passage, if I know it, I would be happy to recite it," he said.

Several people spontaneously raised their hands. One man asked for the soliloquy from *Macbeth.* Another asked for the balcony scene from *Romeo and Juliet.* And then a young woman asked for *Sonnet 14.* One after the other, the actor brought these passages to life—boldly, brilliantly, tenderly, thoughtfully, each excerpt matched perfectly with its corresponding emotion.

Now an elderly gentleman toward the back of the banquet hall raised his hand and the actor called on him. As it turned out, the old man was a priest. "Sir," he said, standing in his place to be heard, "I realize it's not Shakespeare, but I was wondering if you would recite for us the twenty-third Psalm."

The actor paused and looked down as if he were remembering some event far in the past, perhaps a moment in his childhood. Then he smiled and spoke up. "Father, I would be happy to recite the Psalm on just one condition, and that is, when I am finished, you too will recite the Psalm for us here tonight."

The priest was taken aback. He hesitated. He was a little embarrassed now and, looking down, he fidgeted with the tablecloth. But he really wanted to hear the actor recite the Psalm. So finally, he smiled and agreed. "Very well."

The crowd hushed in anticipation and the actor began in his powerful and eloquent voice. "The Lord is my shepherd, there is nothing I shall want . . ."

When the actor finished reciting the Psalm the audience rose to their feet in ovation. They clapped and cheered as if they would never stop, and their adulation again echoed through the castle and out into the midsummer's evening.

After what seemed like several minutes, the guests finally settled and returned to their seats. Then the actor looked down the banquet hall to where the old priest was sitting and said, "Father, it's your turn now."

As the priest stood up at his table a whirl of whispers raced around the room. Shifting in his place, the old priest looked down, placed one hand on the table to steady himself, and took a deep breath.

A look of vivid recollection came across his face. He seemed to slip away to some other place. Then in a voice that was gentle and deeply reflective, he began.

"The Lord is my shepherd,
there is nothing I shall want.
He lets me lie down in green pastures.
He leads me beside peaceful waters.
He restores my soul.
He guides me along the way of righteousness as befits his name.
Even though I walk through
the valley of the shadow of death,
I will not be afraid. For the Lord is at my side. His rod and his
staff comfort and protect me.
He prepares a table for me in the presence of my enemies.
He anoints my head with oil.
My cup overflows.
Surely goodness and mercy will follow me all the days of my life.
And I will live in the house of the Lord, forever."

When the priest was finished not a sound could be heard in the banquet hall. Nobody clapped, nobody moved, and nobody spoke. A profound silence had descended upon the castle. Women wiped tears from their eyes. Men sat staring openmouthed. A tear slipped from the eye of the host. And as the humble old priest gently sat down, every set of eyes in the banquet hall was fixed upon him.

The faces of the guests radiated awestruck amazement. The actor was perplexed. He wondered why the priest's gentle words had touched the people so deeply. Then like a shaft of light passing across his face, it dawned on him.

Seizing the moment, the actor stood up and said, "My friends, do you realize what you have witnessed here tonight?" They gazed back at him with a communal stare of wonderment. They knew they had witnessed something profound, but were uncertain of its meaning. The actor continued, "Why was the old priest's recital of the Psalm so much more powerful than my own? As I see it, the difference is this: I know the Psalm, but Father, he knows the Shepherd."

Get to know the Shepherd. Stop trying to put together a master plan for your life and for your happiness. Instead, seek out the Master's plan for your life and for your happiness. Allow him to lead you, to guide you, to be your companion, your friend, your coach, and your mentor. He will lead you to green pastures. He will restore your soul. And your cup will overflow.

Chapter Three

THE MASS

The Mass is at the center of Catholic tradition, and yet, the general consensus today seems to be that the Mass is boring. We have become used to hearing children say, "I don't want to go to Church. Mass is boring!" Children have been saying this for generations. The disturbing reality is that more and more adults are saying, "Mass is boring!" "It's not relevant to my modern life!" "I don't get anything out of it!" This is now a multi-generational problem, and one that deserves our urgent attention.

On any given Sunday if I look around church I see a large number of men, women, and children who are disengaged. Not distracted at moments, but massively disengaged throughout the whole Mass. We have been talking about this problem for longer than I have been alive. Some people say the problem with the Mass is the way the altar servers behave, others say the problem is that the music is too modern or too old-fashioned, while still others say that the problem with the Mass is the readers, the Eucharistic ministers, the parking lot, the coffee they serve after Mass, or their priest's homilies. We have tried to make Mass more engaging by changing things, adding things, and involving more and more people, but despite all of this, an increasing number of people have stopped attending Mass on a regular basis and profess to be bored or actively disengaged during Mass.

In truth, there is no problem with the Mass. People of all places and times have found it to be the life-transforming centerpiece of their spiritual lives. It has nothing to do with age. Many people, young and old, still find the Mass to be an experience that provides incredible spiritual comfort and clarity. I am one of them. So I am simply unable to accept that the Mass is boring. I am not willing to accept that it is irrelevant to our lives, though I do think we need to consider if our lives are irrelevant to the Mass. I am, however, willing to accept that many, many people are bored at Mass. They have no reason to lie. If they were not bored, I am convinced that they would not say that they were. The question is: How do we move them beyond their boredom to a richer experience of the Mass?

The Mass is not boring, but many people are bored when they go to Mass. This is the essential dilemma we face as a Church. What is the answer? How do we demonstrate the powerful relevance of the Mass? I have studied it for years and have come to the conclusion that two things are necessary if we are to demonstrate the powerful relevance of the Mass to Catholics today.

First, there needs to be a change in the way we approach Mass each Sunday. Every day God is speaking in our lives. The Sunday liturgy is an opportunity for us to take time to listen. We need to teach and learn real and practical ways of listening to God's voice.

Second, we need a renewed understanding of the workings of the Mass and how they relate to our daily lives. Most people know so little about the Mass that it might as well be in a foreign language. Very few Catholics have a working knowledge of what is actually happening at each moment during the Mass. We need to bring the Eucharistic experience to life for people.

In this chapter I will seek to give you some practical insight on both of these points. There are more than a billion Catholics on the planet. The central experience of Catholicism is the Mass, and I believe that we have an obligation together as a Church to engage people. I hope this chapter can be a powerful first step.

• Prepare Yourself •

You wouldn't show up to play in a football game and expect to win if you had not been training. You wouldn't show up unprepared to give a big presentation at work and expect to get the project. We don't expect to excel in exams if we have not studied. Consider the preparation that goes into hosting a BBQ, a dinner party, or a wedding. We prepare for everything we consider important in life. In every case preparation makes a wonderful experience possible. When was the last time you prepared for Mass?

The first step is preparation. It is necessary for a high-level experience. It is unreasonable to walk through the church doors as the music is beginning on Sunday and expect to have a powerful and personal spiritual experience without some preparation.

When does Mass begin for you? For my wife, Meggie, and me, Sunday Mass begins on Wednesday evening. I would like to say we do it every Wednesday, but sometimes we forget and other times we are too lazy. I can tell you that our best experiences of Sunday liturgy come when we have diligently taken a few minutes on Wednesday night to prepare.

Our process is very simple. We read through the Mass readings for the following Sunday, we talk about what strikes us from each of the readings and why, and then we each close with a spontaneous personal prayer. It takes about fifteen minutes, but it places the readings of the coming Sunday in our minds several days before we attend Mass. It's simple, it's powerful, and I encourage you to try it. Do it with your spouse, with your whole family, with some friends, or do it alone. But find a way to prepare for Mass.

Every Sunday we get to experience the Word of God at Mass. I believe the Word of God has the power to transform our lives. I have experienced this power in my own life and witnessed it in the lives of countless others. I believe the Word of God can have a powerful impact in your life right now, beginning today. But I am equally convinced that the Word of God will not transform your life, or mine, with one quick reading on a Sunday morning in a church full of people, where we are surrounded by a thousand distractions. In order to deliver its soothing waters to our souls, the Word of God needs an opportunity to linger in our minds and to sink its roots deep into our hearts. This simply cannot take place in the context of Sunday Mass.

The priest stands up to read the Gospel and everyone in church rises to their feet. At that moment, you get distracted by who is at church or who is not at church, by what someone is wearing or what someone is not wearing, by a child running up and down the aisle throwing his crayons and eating a snack, or throwing his snack and eating his crayons. The point is, you get distracted. The next thing you know, the priest is beginning his homily. You have no idea what the Gospel was about and you go home spiritually undernourished.

Allow me a question to make my point. What was last Sunday's Gospel reading? Do you know? Do you have to think about it? Is it coming to you? Maybe you know and maybe you don't. My experience has been that more than ninety percent of Catholics can't tell you what last Sunday's Gospel was about.

For many people, their only experience of the Scriptures is during Sunday Mass. If we don't know what last Sunday's Gospel reading was, only a few days later, then I have to believe that it didn't significantly impact our lives.

Let me offer you the first practical resolution that will radically improve your experience of Mass on Sunday and your relationship with God. Preparation may be the most powerful tool at your disposal to improve your experience of the Mass. We have spoken about the value of preparation in business, at school, and in sports, so why wouldn't the same truth apply when it comes to Mass? Preparation elevates every worthwhile human endeavor.

I would like to suggest that once a week, perhaps on Tuesday or Wednesday, you take time to read and reflect upon the coming Sunday's Gospel. Just start with the Gospel. Perhaps in time you will move on to reflect on all of the readings, but for now, just start with the Gospel. If you are married, you may wish to share this experience with your spouse. Don't just rush through it. Read next Sunday's Gospel slowly and pick out a word or a phrase that strikes you or jumps out at you. Take turns reading and then explaining which word jumped out at you. Then read through it again. Again, be attentive for a word or phrase that strikes you. Maybe it will be the same word; maybe it will be a different word. It doesn't matter. Read the passage three times. If the Word of God is to transform us we need to allow it to sink its roots deep into our lives through repetition and reflection.

Each time, think about why that particular word or phrase is prodding you. Is there something happening in your life that this word or phrase speaks to? Is there something you should be doing that makes this word or phrase prick your conscience? Perhaps there is something you shouldn't be doing, and this word convicts you. That can be uncomfortable. Or maybe a word comforts you. Inspires you. Let the Holy Spirit work in you.

When you familiarize yourself with next Sunday's Gospel, the Mass will no longer be just part of your routine. It will become a spiritual experience and part of your own personal adventure of salvation.

We love what we know. When you get into the car, what songs do you want to hear on the radio? Songs you know. When you go to the theater, what language do you want the play to be in? The language you know.

If you apply this one resolution to your life, and practice it with an open, honest, and humble heart, your whole experience of Mass on Sunday will improve tremendously. And little by little, you will begin to draw closer to the man whose footprints have left an indelible mark in the dusty paths of human history.

The Word of God needs opportunities to linger in our hearts and minds. If we give it these opportunities it will move like running water toward the cracks in our lives. These cracks are our questions and heartaches, and God wants to speak directly to them. Only then will the powerful and personal modern relevance of God's ageless wisdom become unquestionably apparent in our modern lives.

Taking a few minutes during the week to prepare is the first step toward a more engaging experience of Mass each Sunday. Beyond that, turning the radio off as we drive to Church and arriving a few minutes early to consciously place ourselves in the presence of God are simple, practical ways to prepare for Mass. Find what works for you and make it a habit.

• Get Yourself a Mass Journal •

Having prepared ourselves for Mass, the next step is to approach Mass with an open heart and open mind—expecting God to communicate with us. While many people complain about being bored at Mass, I have to believe that most Catholics would like to have a richer experience of it each Sunday. With that in mind I would like to propose a simple approach that I think could change the whole way we experience the Mass, and at the same time transform our relationships and parishes.

When you walk into Mass next Sunday, simply ask God in the quiet of your heart, *God, show me one way in this Mass that I can become a-better-version-of-myself this week!* Then listen. A critical component of successful relationships that is missing from our spiritual lives is listening. Listen to what God is saying to you in the music, through the readings, in the homily. Listen to the prayers of the Mass, and listen to the quiet of your heart. The one thing will strike you. Once it is revealed to you, spend the rest of the Mass praying about how you can live that one thing in the coming week.

Better than that, sometime this week, go out and get yourself a small journal. Bring it home and write down inside the front cover, "God, show me one way in this Mass that I can become a-better-version-of-myself this week!" Not "God, show me one way in this Mass my spouse can become a-better-version-of-him/herself this week!" Not "God, show me one way in this Mass my children can become better-versions-of-themselves this week!" No, God will speak to your spouse and your children in his own time and in a way that is specific to them. For now, the request you are laying before God is, "God, show me one way in this Mass that I can become a-better-version-of-myself this week!"

Then bring that journal to Church with you on Sunday. Try to arrive a few minutes early for Mass. Place this request before God: *Show me one way in this Mass that I can become a-better-version-of-myself this week!* Then listen to the music, the readings, the prayers of the Mass, the homily, the quiet of your heart. When that one thing strikes you, write it in your Mass Journal. Now spend the rest of the Mass praying about how you can become a-better-version-of-yourself in that way during the coming week.

If you do that every Sunday for a year your Mass Journal will become an incredibly powerful spiritual tool. You will be able to take it to your daily prayer and pass from page to page. Each page will inspire a deeply personal dialogue between you and God.

For many years now I have been doing just this at Mass each Sunday.

It is usually fairly simple things that God says to me in these pages: "Avoid using negative humor." "Cherish your wife." "Take time each day to be grateful." "What are you holding back from God?" Each entry provides a unique and personal opportunity for prayer and for growth.

But perhaps the most powerful aspect of this Mass Journal has been the way it subtly tracks our progress. Consider this question: Are you a-better-version-of-yourself today than you were a year ago? Most people cannot answer, or they really have to think about it. But once you have kept your Mass Journal for a year or many years, you will be able to look back and see what you were struggling with a year ago or five years ago, and recognize that you have grown. This is of critical importance, because as human beings we need to know that we are making progress. We need to be able to look in the mirror each night and say, "I'm not perfect, but I am better today than I was yesterday." Even if our progress is only tiny in one area of our lives, it is important that we acknowledge it.

Visit DynamicCatholic.com/massjournal and request a free Mass Journal.

I have said it over and over again, and I will say it some more: Our lives change when our habits change. Get yourself a Mass Journal and bring it to church with you each Sunday. Write down that one thing that God whispers into your soul. This one habit will change your whole experience of the Mass, your relationship with God, and your appreciation of the Church. This one habit will help you become a-better-version-of-yourself, will make you a more engaged and contributing member of your parish community, and will invigorate your relationships.

Now take it a step further. Imagine if every person in your parish came to church each Sunday with a Mass Journal looking for one way they could become a-better-version-of-themselves in the coming week. Imagine the conversations you could have with your spouse, your children, your pastor, your friends.

And finally, take it one more step. There are more than sixty-five million Catholics in the United States. Imagine if every one of them came to church each Sunday with a Mass Journal looking for one way they could become a-better-version-of-themselves in the coming week. This one habit alone is powerful and practical enough to awaken a hunger for continuous learning, a desire for best practices, and a willingness to listen to the voice of God in our lives. This single habit is practical and powerful enough to transform the entire Church.

Our lives change when our habits change. Our relationships change when our habits within those relationships change. Our families change when our habits as families change. And our Church will change and become the invigorated life-giving community God intends it to be when our habits as members of the Church support that mission.

I believe that God is constantly speaking to us, through people and events, through the Scriptures and the Church. But each Sunday we have an intimate encounter with God in the Mass. Perhaps here more than anywhere else, God wants to speak to you. If you believed God was going to speak to you at Mass, I suspect you would bring pen and paper. Get yourself a Mass Journal.

• Rediscovering the Mass •

I offer the concept of a Mass Journal as a starting point. This single habit is enough to completely alter the way we approach Mass because it opens us up to listening to the voice of God in our lives. It is also a great place to begin because you can activate it now. You already know enough to practice this habit, you don't need years of study to understand it, and it is not dependent on good music, an outstanding homily, or any other variable factor surrounding the Mass. It depends only upon you opening yourself to listen to the voice of God in your life. So it provides a wonderful starting point, but as I said earlier, two things are necessary if we are going to invigorate our experience of the Mass: a change in the way we approach Mass each Sunday, and a renewed understanding of the workings of the Mass and how they relate to our daily lives. These new habits of preparing for Mass and keeping a Mass Journal will radically alter the way most people approach Mass each Sunday, but we also need to move toward a deeper understanding of what we are actually witnessing, experiencing, and participating in at Mass.

During the life and times of Francis of Assisi religion had become more of a habit and empty tradition than a genuine conviction. Just as in the time of Francis of Assisi, for many modern Catholics Mass (and the practice of religion) has become more of a habit and a social gathering than an expression of any genuine spiritual conviction.

On my way to Mass, I often reflect on the idea that if Muslims believed that God was truly present in their mosques, and that by some mystical power they could receive and consume him in the form of bread and wine, they would crawl over red-hot broken glass for the chance. But as Catholics, we are so unaware of the mystery and the privilege that most of us cannot be bothered to show up to church on Sunday and many of those who do can hardly wait to get out.

Modern Catholics complain about the Mass in a constant litany: "Mass is boring." "The music is too old-fashioned." "I couldn't understand what the priest was trying to say." "The sound system is no good." "It went for too long." "I cannot relate to the priest." "The people at Mass are not my age." Maybe, just maybe, we are missing the point.

It seems we have lost our sense of wonder. This is true in almost every area of our lives, but particularly when it comes to matters of faith and spirituality. We have lost the quintessential quality of childhood—wonder.

Do you experience the wonder? Are you able to look beyond what appear to be routine actions of the Mass to the timeless meaning? Do you sense the mystery and power of receiving and consuming Christ in the Eucharist? Do you marvel at the fact? If we believe that Christ is truly present in the Eucharist, then the power unleashed within us by the consumption of the Eucharist is immeasurable.

I often wonder as I watch great athletes compete, knowing that they are not Catholic, how much better they would perform if they believed Christ was present in the Eucharist and they could receive him right before a race. What is true for these athletes is also true for our lives. There is incredible power in the Eucharist.

We don't go to Mass to socialize. We don't go to be entertained. We go to give ourselves to God, and in return to receive God. Open your heart, open your mind, and open your soul to the miracles God wants to work in and through you.

Life is not about what sort of shoes you wear. It's not about what street you live on. It is not about how much money you have in the bank or what sort of car you drive. It's not about whether or not you get that promotion, or where you and your family vacation each year. Life is not about whom you have dated, whom you are dating, or whom you married. It is not about whether or not you made the football team. Life is not about what college you went to, what college may or may not accept you, or what college your children are going to. Life isn't about these things.

Life is about whom you love and whom you hurt. Life is about how you love yourself and how you hurt yourself. It's about how you love and hurt the people in your life. You can't see these things, but they are powerful and real.

Mass is not about whom you sit next to. It's not about which priest says Mass. It is not about what you wear or who is there. Mass is not about the music. It's not even about the preaching. It is about gathering as a community to give thanks to God for all the blessings he fills our lives with. It is about receiving the body and blood of Christ, not just physically, but spiritually. Perhaps you have been receiving the Eucharist physically every Sunday for your whole life. Next Sunday, prepare yourself, be conscious of the marvel, the wonder, the mystery, and receive spiritually.

Rediscover the wonder.

• A Quick Journey Through the Mass •

As I work my way through these seven chapters covering the Seven Pillars of Catholic Spirituality I have paused time and time again and thought, *I really need a whole book to explain each pillar.* Each time I fall into this pattern of thought I have to remind myself that my intent here is to give you an overall perspective of Catholicism and what it could mean to your life, while at the same time whetting your appetite and inspiring you to take the next step in your journey. I hope spiritual reading will become a daily part of your life after you read this book, and that this is the first of many spiritual books you will read.

With this in mind, I would now like to take you on a quick journey through the various parts of the Mass. In doing so, I hope to unveil some of the meanings that too often remain unknown and hidden, and instruct you about ways you can become more actively engaged throughout the Mass.

Introductory Rites. These essentially consist of the entrance procession and song, a greeting, the Sign of the Cross, the penitential act, the Gloria, and an opening prayer.

Entrance. After the people are assembled the entrance song begins. Like every single part of the Mass, the opening song and procession have intended meaning. This song opens the celebration. It is designed to bind us together as a community, to intensify our unity. The song should also be carefully selected to lead our thoughts to the mystery of the particular feast or season.

Engage: Make an effort to sing. You may not enjoy singing, or you may be unable to sing. In that case, follow the words of the song in your hymnal, reflecting on how they challenge or comfort you.

Penitential Act. This is the moment when we acknowledge that some of our thoughts, words, and actions have not helped us become the-best-version-of-ourselves, have prevented other people from being all God created them to be, and ultimately have created an obstacle between us and the infinite love of God.

Engage: Identify a specific thought, word, or action that created an obstacle between you and God this week and ask forgiveness.

Gloria. *Glory to God in the highest and on earth peace to people of good will . . .* The Gloria is an ancient hymn that praises God. Our earthly relationships have become very transactional. We tend to speak to people only when we want something or if they have done something wrong. This transactional mentality has overflowed into our spiritual lives, and as a result the practice of praising God has fallen largely into disuse.

Engage: Set yourself and your life aside for a moment, and praise God for something specific. Praise God for his goodness. Praise God for creation. Praise God for his wisdom.

Opening Prayer. This is one of my favorite parts of the Mass. I find the opening prayers to be ever fresh and phenomenally profound. They also provide a prelude to what we are about to hear and experience. The opening prayer is designed to place us in the presence of God and focus our hearts and minds. This is the opening prayer from the twenty-first week of Ordinary Time: *Father, help us to seek the values that will bring us lasting joy in this changing world. In our desire for what you promise, make us one in mind and heart.* The opening prayers of the Mass guide us to focus on the themes that will emerge in the readings that day. This is the opening prayer for Friday during the fourth week of Lent: *Father, our source of life, you know our weakness. May we reach out with joy to grasp your hand and walk more readily in your ways.*

Engage: Get yourself a missal and begin to follow the prayers of the Mass.

Liturgy of the Word. This essentially consists of the Scripture readings, homily, profession of faith, and the general intercessions.

Scripture Readings. The readings that make up the Liturgy of the Word for Sunday Mass include an Old Testament reading, a responsorial Psalm, a New Testament reading, and a Gospel reading. The readings are not randomly selected; they are related to each other in some way, and belong to a flow that moves us from the readings last week to the readings next week.

Engage: Take time during the week to read over and reflect upon next Sunday's readings. Find the readings in your Bible and underline them. Over time this will give you a sense of the parts of the Bible you have experienced.

Homily. The average homily lasts approximately seven minutes and for many people this is the only exposure they have to religious education all week. This is the priest's moment to speak to the community—and a singular opportunity to nurture Christian life. The challenge the priest faces is to develop some point from the readings and transform it into a powerful teaching moment. Jesus always met people where they were, and from there he led them to a better life. The homily is the priest's opportunity to convince people that Jesus has answers to the issues and questions they are struggling with, and that the life Jesus invites us to is simply the best way to live.

Engage: As a lay participant in the Mass the homily is largely outside of your control. But more often than not God uses a single phrase to speak to us. Listen. Stay open to what God might be trying to say to you. On many occasions I have attended Mass in foreign countries where I had no knowledge of the language, and yet God has spoken to me powerfully.

Our Profession of Faith. This is where we proclaim our faith as individuals and as a community. If you really reflect on the Creed I suspect you will have questions or doubts almost every time you say it. Those doubts and questions are invitations to explore and study our faith more, but also to place our trust in God and his Church. I used to find it comforting when we pray together, "We believe . . ." (before they changed it to "I believe") because whatever was lacking in what I believed on any given Sunday (because of doubts and questions that I may have) was made up for by the faith of someone in the pew in front of me or behind me, on the other side of town or the other side of the world. Together we have a complete faith.

Engage: Whatever you have questions or doubts about in the Creed, begin to explore them vigorously, one at a time. Examine why the Church teaches what she teaches in each instance and allow your questions and doubts to strengthen your faith rather than diminish it.

General Intercessions. The Mass is the most powerful prayer in human history. At every moment of every day, a Mass is taking place somewhere, and we (the Catholic Church) are praying for the entire human family. This is really quite beautiful if you stop and think about it. At this point of the Mass we offer specific intentions to God as a community. These usually include a prayer for the Church, a prayer for world leaders, prayers for those who are oppressed and those in need, prayer for the local community, and others.

Engage: Consider whom and what you are praying for. Immerse yourself for a moment in that person's need, responsibilities, or pain.

The Collection. At this time a basket is passed so that we can contribute financially to the mission of the Church. What we place in the basket we are giving to God and to the needy. It is a real and practical expression of loving God and neighbor. These funds are used to cover the expenses of the Church and the various ministries that the community is involved in.

Engage: Give generously—not because your parish needs the money, not because the priest gave a good homily, and not because others might know what you gave. Give generously because we have a real and present spiritual need to give. We also need to guard against the allure of money. It is easier to trust money than it is to trust God. "In God we trust," it says on our money. But do we? This regular Sunday giving is a sign of letting go, a sign of surrender. Too often in our society we give with lots of strings attached. Often I hear people say, "I don't give to the Church because I don't like how they spend the money." Whether this is true or not in any particular situation, this statement is filled with judgment and generalization, the pride that we know better, and a desire to control. These are all the behaviors that spiritual giving is designed to liberate us from. Give generously. It is hard, I know. You will feel torn; such is the pull of money in our lives.

Liturgy of the Eucharist. This is the "center and the summit of the entire celebration" and consists of the Eucharistic prayer, Consecration, the Our Father and sign of peace, and Communion.

The Offertory. Representatives from the community bring forward the bread and wine, along with our offerings for the Church and the poor. At the same time, the priest and servers are preparing the altar for our offering.

Engage: As the gifts are being brought forward and as the priest is preparing the gifts, in your heart bring the different aspects of your life forward and offer them to God. Offer God your marriage, your family, your career, your business, your friendships. In a special way offer him your successes and failures. Hold up to God a friend who is suffering in some way. Offer him a particular struggle that you are enduring. Offer God everything. Mentally and spiritually place them all on the altar so that God can transform them.

Eucharistic Prayer. The word *Eucharist* means "thanksgiving." During this sequence of prayers the priest invites us to lift up our hearts to the Lord. In this way, we are offering ourselves with Jesus to God the Father. This prayer also reminds us of God's goodness and his friendship with humanity throughout history.

Engage: Bring the words to life. Live them out. With your spiritual senses, lift up your heart and offer it to the Lord. Place your heart on the altar and allow God to transform it as he will transform the bread and wine.

The Consecration. Leading up to the consecration, the priest recites the narrative of the Last Supper connecting what we experience in every Mass with Jesus' institution of the Eucharist. The actual consecration is the moment when the bread and wine become the body and blood of Jesus Christ. This happens when the priest recites the words of Jesus over them: "This is my body which is given up for you; this is the blood of the new and everlasting covenant, do this in memory of me."

Engage: Simply allow yourself to be in the presence of God. Quiet your mind. Imagine yourself close to Jesus at the Last Supper or at the Crucifixion. Then as the priest elevates the host and the chalice, say with Thomas in your heart, "My Lord and my God." These mysteries are mysteries, but if we approach them humbly, often, and with reverence, God will give us an ever-increasing love and understanding of them.

The Lord's Prayer. Now we join together as a community to pray in the way that Jesus taught us.

Engage: You have prayed these words a thousand times before, but allow them to be new and fresh. Focus on a particular word or phrase and allow it to permeate your whole being. If you are struggling to cooperate with God's will perhaps you will focus on *thy will be done.* Or maybe you have real and human needs that are not being met, so your focus may fall on the words *give us this day our daily bread.* Perhaps you feel the need to be forgiven for something you have said or done: *forgive us our trespasses.* Maybe you need the grace to forgive someone who has wronged you: *as we forgive those who trespass against us.* Or perhaps you are struggling with a particular temptation at this time in your life: *lead us not into temptation, but deliver us from evil.*

Sign of Peace. The priest has asked God to grant us peace and unity. Nobody needs to be reminded of how fractured our world and Church have become, which makes this an especially powerful moment in the liturgy. Here we embrace the whole world. Jesus has loved us in this Eucharist by sharing his peace with us, and now we share the peace and love of Christ with those around us. This is symbolic of the way we are called to take the peace and love of Jesus out into the world.

Engage: Everybody has had their heart broken by something or someone. Jesus wants to soothe and heal our broken heart. He offers his peace to you to heal your broken heart and invites you to pass that peace on to others. As you offer the sign of peace to those around you at Mass be mindful that while they may look happy and seem like they have it all together, we all have a broken heart that needs healing.

Communion. This is the moment when we receive the body and blood of Jesus Christ in the form of bread and wine. It is almost beyond belief, and many have left the Church, just as many left Jesus in his own time, because of this single teaching: "This teaching is just too difficult." (John 6:60)

Engage: As you approach the altar to receive Communion be mindful of what is about to take place. I pray this short prayer over and over to allow me to focus on what is happening: *I wish, my Lord, to receive you as generously as your holy mother Mary did.*

Thanksgiving. These moments of reflection after receiving the Eucharist can be extremely powerful if we make ourselves present to them. The fruits of Holy Communion include unity with Jesus, nourishment for the spiritual life, a hunger for virtue, a desire to do the will of God, cleansing from past sins, a fanning of the flames of Christian love, grace to avoid sin in the future, sensitivity to the promptings of the Holy Spirit, and a desire to know God more intimately.

Engage: For these precious moments when Christ is so mysteriously present in you, kneel or sit, close your eyes, and just thank God in your own words for all the blessings in your life. Name them specifically—people, places, things, and opportunities that you are grateful for. Allow your heart to fill and overflow with gratitude.

Concluding Rites. The concluding rites are made up of the final blessing and the dismissal.

Final Blessing. On the way into church we blessed ourselves with the Sign of the Cross. Before the Gospel we blessed our mind, our lips, and our heart. Now we receive a blessing.

Engage: Bow your head, close your eyes, and allow the words of the final blessing to penetrate the very depths of your being.

The Dismissal. The Mass takes its name from this final statement: "Go in peace, glorifying the Lord by your life." *Ite, missa est* is a Latin phrase that means "Go, you are sent."

Engage: In this final moment of the Mass we are being sent on a mission to light up the ways of this world with the love of Christ, a love that is willing to sacrifice for others, a love that knows no limits. As you leave Church and return to the world, consider how you might live out your Christian mission this week.

There is incredible genius and beauty in the Mass, but to discover it we need to be constantly delving into it a little deeper. At every moment of the Mass there are rich opportunities to engage personally in the experience, thus transforming it from a monotonous ritual into a deeply relevant and ever-changing experience of God.

I have taken just a few minutes to give you a glimpse of the depth, the beauty, and the relevance of what we knowingly or unknowingly witness at church every Sunday. Now let us make the journey from being mere witnesses and become actively engaged participants.

• Spiritual Game Changer •

Working as business consultants, my partners and I are often asked by clients to help them identify what would be a "game changer" for their business. As I was engaged in this process with a client a few weeks ago I started to wonder, *What would be a game changer for my spiritual life?* This led me to reflect on what had been the game changers in the past. The first was definitely when I started spending ten minutes a day at church on the way to school. The second was the first time I really read the Gospels. The third was my first regular experience of daily Mass.

I didn't go every day, but a couple of months after I started spending ten minutes at church each morning, I began attending Mass on Tuesday evenings at my parish in Sydney. It was at Mass during the week that I discovered the genius of it. It was at these quiet and intimate daily Mass experiences that this sacred ritual really began to ignite my love for Catholicism. I would follow the opening prayer, the readings, and the closing prayer in my missal, and the words began to probe my heart and ignite the fire in my soul.

I would walk down to church and it would be just me, the priest, and about ten other men and women much older than I was. It was quiet, peaceful, and intimate. It was there in that daily Mass experience that I fell in love with the Mass, and the Church. By some grace, I started to listen to the prayers of the Mass, really listen . . . and it was like the pieces of a puzzle coming together to form an incredible vision.

The Mass reveals God's vision for us as individuals, his vision for marriage and family, for community and society, and for the Church and the world.

There is genius and beauty in the prayers of the Mass, and yet, most people tune out the prayers. It seems to me that keeping God's dream for us to become the-best-version-of-ourselves in the forefront of our mind unlocks the language of the many prayers that make up the Mass.

The prayers of the Mass remind us that we are pilgrims on a journey, that we are not on this journey alone, and that we are called to be responsible stewards of our own lives while at the same time living in a way that is mindful of the needs of others and mindful of the needs of all of creation. Over and over again, the prayers of the Mass orient us toward God and remind us of his desire to have a relationship with us.

There is great beauty in these prayers, but too often we don't hear them because we are distracted by our thoughts or by those around us. Some of the prayers are the same for every Mass. Others change with the seasons of the Church calendar. And still others change every day. If you take time to listen and truly pray these prayers as the priest says them, you will discover the intimate knowledge the Church has of our spiritual needs.

I will be the first to admit that at times it is difficult to concentrate on these prayers during the Mass. For that reason, I would encourage you to get yourself a missal. It may seem a little old-fashioned to some people, but owning a missal took my understanding and appreciation of the Mass to a whole new level. If you don't want to carry around a large missal, get yourself a subscription to *Word Among Us* or *Magnificat*. These are small monthly prayer companions that have morning prayer, the readings and prayers for Mass each day, evening prayer, and a variety of inspirational spiritual readings. They are very powerful spiritual tool in our busy times.

Visit DynamicCatholic.com/missal to order your subscription.

The prayers of the Mass are beautifully integrated and carefully designed to keep us focused on God's dream for us to become the-best-version-of-ourselves. For example, the opening prayer on the second week of Ordinary Time is: *Almighty and ever-present Father, your watchful care reaches to the ends of the earth and orders all things in such power that even the tension and tragedies of sin cannot frustrate your loving plans. Help us to embrace your will, give us the strength to follow your call, so that your truth may live in our hearts and reflect peace to those who believe in your love.* The opening prayers of the Mass guide us to focus on the themes that will emerge in the readings that day. This is the opening prayer for the Thursday after Ash Wednesday: *Lord, may everything we do begin with your inspiration, continue with your help, and reach perfection under your guidance.*

Get yourself a missal and just begin to follow the opening prayer, the readings, and the closing prayer, and your experience of the Mass will increase exponentially. Then during the week, begin a habit of going to Mass once or twice. This more intimate experience of the sacrament will truly fan the fire of your soul. On the days when you don't attend Mass, use the prayers and the readings from Mass that day during your time of prayer. And once in your life you should try to go to Mass every day for a whole week. Try it; you will be amazed.

Our lives change when our habits change. The only way for the Church to become more spiritual is for the people who make up the Church to become more spiritual. We become more spiritual when we seek the will of God by establishing spiritual habits. This is one real and practical way to unearth the riches of Catholicism in our day-to-day lives.

• My Favorite Prayer •

Do you have a favorite prayer in the Mass? My favorite is right before the sign of peace, when the priest prays, *Deliver us, Lord, from every evil and grant us peace in our days. In your mercy keep us free from sin, and protect us from all anxiety as we wait in joyful hope for the coming of our Savior, Jesus Christ.*

These words mean so much to me. To live a life free from sin is a humble and simple ambition, but a noble one. There is an Australian song I remember from my childhood titled *Tenterfield Saddler*. It's about a man named George who lived in a small country town. All day long he would sit on his verandah making horse saddles, and over the years he became a sage-like figure for the locals. The song begins:

The late George Woolnough
Worked on High Street
Lived on manners
For fifty-two years he sat on his verandah
And made his saddles.

And if you had questions
About sheep or flowers or dogs
You just asked the saddler
He lived without sin
They're building a library for him.

The line that arrests me is *He lived without sin*. I have seen how sin complicates our lives, confuses our minds, and hardens our hearts. I have seen the devastating effects of sin in my own life, in the lives of the people I love, and in the lives of complete strangers. I want to live a life free from sin, and the prayer *keep us free from sin* resonates with the deepest desires of my heart. I love the peace that is the fruit of a clear conscience. The truth is, the happiest times of my life have been when I was actively trying to live free from sin.

Protect us from all anxiety—all anxiety, not some anxiety. How much of our lives do we waste worrying? A friend of mine has a quote by Corrie ten Boom on her answering machine that says, "Worry doesn't empty tomorrow of its suffering; it empties today of its strength."

I know it is the sin in my life that causes my pain, anguish, impatience, anxiety, irritableness, restlessness, and discontentment. We waste so much time and energy on sin. Imagine how much you and I could accomplish if we didn't waste so much time and energy on sin!

It is also during the Mass that we are reminded of the good, kind, and gentle love of God as Father, as we join together before Communion to pray the Our Father.

A good friend of mine volunteers in Chicago prisons, visiting the inmates and leading Bible studies. Not too long ago, he invited me to visit a maximum-security facility and speak to the prisoners. I accepted the invitation, and a couple of weeks before the event was scheduled to take place, I asked to speak with the three chaplains from the prison to get a sense of the group. They told me many things about the group, but the most alarming fact they shared was in relation to the entire male prison population in America. In fact, ninety percent of male prisoners in America today between the ages of sixteen and thirty grew up separated from their biological fathers. Ninety percent!

I believe the present fatherless generation is the result of the evil forces that tempt our hearts. You may not be separated from your biological father, but these same evil forces want to sow in you the seeds of doubt, skepticism, and cynicism. And in doing so, they separate you from your heavenly Father.

I don't speak of them often, but I believe evil spirits exist, and that they are at work in the world and in our lives. Like C. S. Lewis, I believe that it is a mistake to give the devil too much attention while it is also a mistake to give the devil too little attention.

The devil wants to orphan you. He wants to drag you away from your Father. He wants to crush the Spirit in you that leads you to cry out to God, *Abba Father*. He wants to kidnap you from your spiritual Father. He wants to distract you from the gentle and persistent call of your heavenly Father. Don't let him. Ponder just those first two words of this ancient prayer: *Our Father*. If we could really understand this single truth of God as Father, we would weep for joy every time this prayer crossed our lips.

I also believe that the liberty and equality that men and women have struggled with and searched for throughout history have been revealed through this simple prayer. If only we could understand and grasp the fact that we are all children of God. Only then can we relate to each other as we should.

The prayers of the Mass are profound and powerful. Rediscover them.

• Beyond You and Me •

The Catholic Church is a family of prayer. At every moment of every day the Mass is being celebrated all over the world and we are praying as Catholics not only for ourselves and our own needs, but for the whole human family.

Beyond our own personal experience of the Mass, it is important to be aware of the much greater scope of it. It is in the Mass that the 1.2 billion Catholics around the world come together to share a common experience. But the wisdom of regular worship has a much deeper meaning than bringing us all together once a week; it is a profound reflection of God's blueprint for all of creation.

I wrote *The Rhythm of Life* not only for a Catholic audience, nor alone for a Christian audience, but for the whole cross section of society. And yet, I learned the premise upon which I based the book from the way the Church structures our practice of Christianity. Everything in creation has rhythm. Rhythm is at the core of God's genius for creation. As we turn to God, we are invited to use this same blueprint for our life. In Genesis, we read that God created the world in six days and rested on the seventh. He didn't rest because he was tired. God rested on the seventh day because he foresaw our need for rest.

The seasons change to a rhythm. The tides come in and go out to a rhythm. The sun rises and sets to a rhythm. Your heart pumps blood through your body to a rhythm. Plants grow according to the process of photosynthesis, which is based on a rhythm. And ultimately, the workings of a woman's body are based on a rhythm—and that rhythm gives forth new life. The rhythm gives birth to harmony, efficiency, effectiveness, health, happiness, peace, and prosperity. Destroy the rhythm and you invite chaos, confusion, destruction, and disorder.

This is the wisdom upon which the Church bases our worship as Catholics. The Church bases the calendar on the rhythm that God has placed at the center of creation. In turn, the Church hopes this will help us to place this essential rhythm at the center of our own lives.

It is within this context that we can begin to understand Sunday as a day of rest and renewal, and more specifically, the role of the Mass in the Catholic lifestyle.

• Embrace the Gift •

God doesn't call us to church on Sunday because he has some egotistical need for us all to fall down before him and worship him at ten o'clock each Sunday morning. It isn't designed to help him; it's designed to help us. It isn't intended to make him happy; it's intended to allow us to share in his happiness.

There is a beautiful song titled "Come to the Feast Divine," written by Liam Lawton, from his album *In the Quiet*. Everything about this piece of music invites us to an incredible celebration. It begins with a simple question, "Will you come to the Feast Divine?" I hope you will. I will be there with you in spirit with all the angels and the saints. Pray for me as I pray for you. The Mass is filled with riches. It is an unfathomable gift. Embrace the gift.

Chapter Four

THE BIBLE

The young man's name was Michael. It was a little more than a week before his eighteenth birthday when he stopped by his father's office one day after school. He had been disagreeing with his father about most things lately, and as he walked into the office, Michael said, "Dad, it's going to be my birthday next Tuesday, and if you love me you'll get me a new car for my birthday." His father just looked at him and Michael continued, "And if you really love me, you'll get me the car I've always wanted." Then, without giving his father a chance to reply, he left.

The next morning at breakfast his father said jokingly, "Michael, yesterday when you stopped by the office, you didn't mention what sort of car you've always wanted."

Michael replied, "You know, Dad, a red Porsche."

The boy's father smiled and asked, "And how much do they cost?"

"Ninety-two thousand dollars, and if you really love me, Dad, that's what you'll get me for my birthday. Don't let me down," Michael replied and left for school.

Tuesday came, and as was the family's custom, they celebrated Michael's birthday with dinner and the cutting of the cake. And as they enjoyed their cake, one by one Michael's brothers and sisters handed him a gift. He opened the gifts and thanked them each graciously, but his mind was elsewhere. Finally, the moment he had been waiting for arrived.

Even as Michael's father handed him a small rectangular parcel, he hoped he would find the keys to his new car. Michael ripped at the wrapping paper and discovered that it was a book, a Bible. He didn't even finish unwrapping it. Disgusted, he stood up, pushed his chair away from the table and against the wall behind him, and rushed from the dining room.

Racing upstairs to his bedroom, he slammed the door and threw the still-unopened gift against the wall. It hit the wall, then the floor, and bounced into the corner.

Michael went to bed without talking to anyone. The next morning he got up early and went to school, again without speaking to anyone.

Just before lunch that day, Michael's father suffered a massive heart attack. He was rushed to the hospital, and arrangements were made to bring Michael from school to the hospital to be with his father. For seven hours, Michael sat at his unconscious father's bedside, playing the events of the night before over and over in his head. Exhausted and hungry, he got up and went to get some coffee and a sandwich, and while he was gone his father died.

Michael was devastated. He went home, lay on his bed, and cried. He wept inconsolably for hours, and then out of the corner of his eye he saw the gift, still unopened, sitting in the corner.

Getting up off the bed, he went over and picked it up and finished unwrapping it. For some time he just sat there holding the leather Bible and staring at it. Then, opening the Bible, he discovered an inscription on the inside front cover.

Dear Michael,
Within these pages, you will find the answers to all of life's questions,
and the secrets to all of life's success. With love on your eighteenth
birthday,
Dad

Michael wept some more. The tears streamed down his face, falling to the page and smudging his father's handwriting. To console himself, Michael opened the Bible and flicked through the pages, hoping to find some words to comfort him. What he discovered was that his father had placed a bookmark in the Bible. He removed the bookmark and stared at it with openmouthed amazement.

It was a check for ninety-two thousand dollars.

This father was able to give his son everything from a material standpoint, it seems. But more important, he wanted his son to place the Word of God at the center of his life. His son was surprised to find the check in the Bible, but I hope it was just one of many wonderful surprises he found in its pages.

In the same way, God wants us to discover the many surprises he has tucked away in the pages of the Bible. And, as it was with Michael, we often value the wrong things and set our hearts on our own selfish plans. But God has a better plan for each of our lives than we could even imagine for ourselves, and he always wants to give us more.

• Where Did the Bible Come From? •

Of all the books ever written or published, the Bible is the most widely read, studied, translated, printed, sold, gifted, distributed, and quoted. It is the best-selling book of all time. When it comes to teaching about the nature of God and his desires for us, no other book comes close. In the Bible, we discover the depth and generosity of God's love, as well as his desire to soothe humanity's yearning for truth and happiness. Where did the Bible come from? How did we come to be blessed with such a rare treasure?

I begin our discussion of the Scriptures with these questions because in recent Christian history the Bible has been kidnapped by Protestant and Evangelical Christians.

At one time or another, most Catholics have been cornered by an overzealous Christian in the workplace or supermarket. They immediately start quoting Scripture, and oftentimes their well-argued ideas leave their Catholic targets tired, confused, filled with doubts, and feeling spiritually inadequate. Chances are, if the conversation proceeds to any length, they will approach the idea that the Bible is the one and only source of inspiration, direction, and Revelation. This of course, is a direct attack upon the Catholic Church. It may be carefully masked or subtly presented. Those presenting the idea may not even be aware that it is an attack on Catholicism. But as Catholics, we believe that both the "Sacred Scriptures and sacred tradition form one sacred deposit of the word of God" (*Dei Verbum*). God reveals himself in nature, he reveals himself in the Scriptures, and he reveals himself in the life of the Church.

It is this dynamic interaction between the Scriptures and tradition that keeps the Word alive. If you separate the Scriptures from the living, breathing institution they were entrusted to, they lose their life. This is a major point of contention between Catholics and other non-Catholic Christians. But with this background and as an attempt to shed a little light on this point of contention, let us return to the original question. Where did the Bible come from?

Well, it didn't just drop down from Heaven one fine day, nor did it appear suddenly on the earth, delivered by an angel of God. The Bible was written with some form of primitive inks and pens by people just like you and me. They were divinely inspired in a way that none of us will fully understand in this life, but they were ordinary people with strengths and weaknesses.

The Bible isn't a book. It is a collection of books—seventy-three in all: forty-six in the Old Testament and twenty-seven in the New Testament. Hence the name *Biblia* in Greek, which means "the books" or "library." It is important to note that most Protestant and Evangelical Bibles contain only sixty-six books. It was during the Reformation that non-Catholic Christians removed the following books: Tobit, Judith, Maccabees 1 and 2, Wisdom, Sirach, and Baruch.

It is important to note that for more than fifteen hundred years all Christians were Catholic, and they all accepted these books as part of the Bible. It is also interesting to note that the great majority of non-Catholic Christians have no idea that there are books missing from their Bible, just as all non-Catholic Christians are Protestants, whether they are aware of it or not. Though the great majority could probably not tell you what they are protesting.

The Bible wasn't written all at once, nor was it all written by one person. In fact, one thousand years elapsed between the writing of the book of Genesis and the writing of the book of Revelation.

If you had lived in the court of King David (1000–962 BC), the only parts of what is today the Bible that you would have read are some of the stories from Genesis, the stories of the Exodus, the journey from Egypt to the Holy Land, and the stories of the Israelites settling in the Holy Land that we find in the book of Judges.

The Old Testament was written and compiled between the twelfth century and the second century BC. It is made up of forty-six books, and is divided into three categories: the Pentateuch, the Prophets, and the Writings.

The Pentateuch, which is also known as the Law, Torah, or the Five Books of Moses, consists of the first five books of the Old Testament: Genesis, Exodus, Leviticus, Numbers, and Deuteronomy. This was the embryo of the Bible. The section known as the Prophets includes all the major and minor prophets of the Old Testament. And finally, the Writings section includes the historical documents.

The New Testament was written between AD 45 and AD 150 and includes twenty-seven books. It is made up of four narratives of the life, death, and resurrection of Jesus: the Gospels, a narrative of the apostles' ministries in the early Church; Acts of the Apostles, twenty-one early letters consisting of Christian counsel, instruction, and encouragement; the Epistles; and Revelation, a book of prophecy.

It is perhaps needless to say that the Bible was not originally written in English (though the way some people represent it you might sometimes wonder). The prominent original language of the Old Testament was Hebrew; Greek was the language of the New Testament. What we have today is a translation into English from the original languages of the prophets, apostles, and evangelists.

In every case, it is important for us to realize that the cultures, countries, and times were very different than what we experience today. Some things can mean one thing in one culture and something quite different in another culture. I learned this very quickly as I began to travel from country to country in the earliest years speaking. In our own lives, we experience this in misunderstandings between generations as close as parents and children.

It is also critically important that we remember that the Bible, as we have it now, was not printed at all until almost fifteen hundred years after the birth of Jesus Christ. It is easy to forget in our modern world, where we can print and publish works from home computers and download them to digital devices, that not all eras have enjoyed the luxury and convenience of the printing press. For almost one and a half millennia after the life, death, and Resurrection of Jesus, the only books that existed were handwritten. This certainly places the modern Protestant-Evangelical idea that every person must carry around a Bible in perspective, along with their criticism that Catholics didn't read the Bible before the Reformation.

If you had lived prior to the invention of the printing press, like the men and women of the first fifteen hundred years of Christianity, you would have had no access whatsoever to a physical Bible. This is not because the Church wanted to keep people ignorant, nor was it because Church leaders did not want people reading the Scriptures. It was simply because every single copy of the Bible was an original manuscript that a Catholic monk or friar had laboriously copied onto pages of parchment or vellum. For a millennium and a half Christians learned about the stories that fill the Scriptures from sermons at Mass, by seeing them in stained glass windows, or by watching them performed in mystery plays.

Today, our non-Catholic Christian brothers and sisters place an enormous emphasis on reading and studying the Bible. And while I am in favor of both, it is critical that we do not lose sight of the fact that hundreds of millions of people came to know Christ without ever owning or studying the Bible. Many modern Christians make it sound like it is impossible to receive salvation without a Bible. If that were the case, what happened to the people who lived before the Bible was printed? What happened to the people who lived before it was even written in its present form? How were men and women introduced to Jesus before the sixteenth century? How were the people of foreign lands inspired to live the Christian life before the Bible was available in mass production? It is here, in the gap of most Protestants' understanding of Christian history, that you find the beauty of Catholicism.

Does God have favorites? Did he favor those born after the fifteenth century more than those before? Surely God desired that the countless millions of people who lived before the fifteenth century would know and follow the life and teachings of Jesus. But how could they if they had no Bibles, or had no money to buy Bibles, or could not read the Bible even if they could buy one, or could not understand the Bible even if they could read it?

From the Catholic perspective, salvation is available to the men and women of every age and every culture. Through the teachings of the Church, the people of every land for two thousand years have learned about the life and teachings of Jesus Christ. The people of every place and time have been encouraged to believe and do all that Jesus taught. And in many cases, this great work has been achieved in all corners of the globe without a written or printed Bible.

With this clear and concise understanding of the history of the Scriptures, the Protestant theory of *sola scriptura,* or "the Bible and the Bible alone," self-destructs into the most monumental case of well-argued nonsense in the history of humanity.

Christians of all denominations around the world owe an enormous debt to the Catholic Church. The Catholic Church, inspired and guided by the Holy Spirit, is responsible for the formulation, preservation, and integrity of the Sacred Scriptures. For fifteen hundred years, when there were no Baptists, Lutherans, Pentecostals, Methodists, Anglicans, Evangelicals, Non-denominationals, or any other Christian Church of any type, the Catholic Church preserved the Scriptures from error, saved them from destruction and extinction, multiplied them in every language under the sun, and conveyed the truths they contained to people everywhere. Time and time again, people have tried to manipulate and corrupt these writings—and in some cases have succeeded—but the Catholic Church has preserved a version that is complete and free from human tampering.

It seems strangely paradoxical that so many who claim to love Jesus Christ would be so hostile toward the Church, which has single-handedly protected the records of his life and teachings for so long.

The Bible is the most profound and sublime collection of writings in human history. It therefore goes without saying that these writings are difficult to understand. Individual interpretation of the Bible is a very slippery path that leads people to great confusion, heartache, and distress. The history of Christianity in the past five hundred years is proof enough of this point. This type of approach doesn't promote unity, and always leads to division among Christians. What sadness Christ must feel as he stands witness to the bickering and division of Christian history. After all, in his final prayer he prayed "that all may be one." (John 17:22)

This is why the Catholic Church has, in her wisdom, so vigorously defended her sole right to interpret the meaning of the Scriptures throughout history. The living voice of the Catholic Church stands as a beacon for all men and women of good will, and announces the life and teachings of Jesus Christ with tradition in one hand and the Scriptures in the other.

Ultimately, interpreting the Scriptures comes down to a question of authority. It perhaps is no surprise that the greatest obstacle to Christian unity is also the question of authority. The greatest challenge that faces us, as Christians, in our quest for unity is to free so many from the blind subservience to a book and deliver them to a loving obedience to God alive and present in the one, holy, catholic, and apostolic Church.

• Jesus: The Turning Point in Human History •

Throughout human history, every civilization has reached out to God. Different societies have reached out to God in different ways, and many of them seem strange to us today, but they all point to a single truth: Deep in the heart of every person, there is a desire to know God and a yearning to draw nearer to him. Similarly, at every moment of human history, God has reached out to man. God desires to be with his people.

God's ultimate expression of this reaching out was the coming of Jesus Christ. Born two thousand years ago, Jesus of Nazareth is not a myth or a legend, but a well-documented figure in history. But more than that, he is the Messiah who had been prophesied in the Jewish Scriptures—our Old Testament—and long awaited by the Jewish people. There is evidence to support this claim in his miracles, but ultimately we must each decide for ourselves: Was Jesus a liar, a lunatic, or the Messiah, as he claimed to be? I suppose it is only by that mysterious and wonderful gift of faith that we are able to conclude that Jesus was who he claimed to be.

Every noble human endeavor in history has been a preparation for the coming of Jesus or a response to his life and teachings.

Jesus lived a life on this earth. He ate, he drank, and he walked down the street. Do you know him as a person? Or is he just a historical figure to you? It is crucial that we move beyond the facade of the story of Jesus Christ. We must delve deep into his life and teachings. We must allow his Spirit to flood the thoughts, words, and actions of our daily lives. In order to do all this it is necessary that we come to know the Gospels intimately.

Saint Jerome once wrote, "Ignorance of the Scriptures is ignorance of Christ." The great tragedy in the modern environment is that people know more about their favorite music group or sports players than they do about Jesus Christ. Get to know Jesus. Read the Gospels. Never let a day pass without pondering a few of the precious words in those four books. Don't just race through them. Choose a small section and read it slowly. Reflect on the meaning. Then reread it and ponder those words. Allow the words to penetrate the hardness of your heart. Allow the words of the Gospels to erode your personal prejudices, to wash away your narrow-mindedness, to banish your judgmental tendencies. You don't have to read five chapters a day—just a small passage. But allow the life and teachings of Jesus Christ, alive and present in the Gospels, to sink their roots deep into your life.

Imagine yourself there with dusty sandals, on those hot days, edging just to get a little closer to him, the crowd pressing in on every side. Only then will we form an intimate relationship with this man we call Jesus. Only then will we discover that he is God and Savior, but also coach, companion, mentor, guide, brother, teacher, healer, and friend.

• Where Should You Start? •

There are many ways to approach reading the Bible. You could, of course, start at Genesis and read your way through to Revelation. It is one way to do it and millions of people do it this way every year. They start the year with a resolution to read the Bible, and they do, from start to finish. The primary problem with this approach is that the books are not even placed in chronological order, and so the bigger picture can be lost. The Bible was not assembled to be read from beginning to end.

Start with the Gospels—Matthew, Mark, Luke, and John. Don't just read them once. Read them over and over, fifteen or twenty minutes a day, for a whole year. Allow the life and teachings of Jesus Christ to sink their roots deep into your heart, mind, soul, and life.

You may have read them before, or feel that you have been adequately exposed to them at church. But this passing familiarity with Jesus and the Gospels can actually be a disadvantage. It can lead us to overlook the radical nature of Jesus' teachings. The teachings of Jesus Christ were radical two thousand years ago, and they are just as radical today. If you doubt that, consider Matthew 5:44: "Love your enemies and pray for those who persecute you." Before this, what had been the teaching? An "eye for an eye, tooth for a tooth." (Exodus 21:24) It is easy to read this teaching and accept it intellectually, but living it requires a constant vigilance.

Unless we are willing to constantly examine the way we live, love, work, think, and speak under the piercing light of the Gospels, we will almost certainly find ourselves gradually adopting a Gospel of convenience. A Gospel of convenience consists of, taking what we find easy and comfortable from the teachings of Jesus and ignoring the rest.

For example, let us consider the teaching, "Love your enemies and pray for those who persecute you." Each year I visit more than one hundred cities in the regular course of my work, and so I have the opportunity to attend many different parishes for Mass throughout the year. In the course of the Mass we pray for many people. We pray for the sick, the addicted, the hungry, the lonely, the depressed, the marginalized, the dead, and many others. But since September 11, 2001, I have not heard a single prayer in any of our Churches for Osama bin Laden, or for Al Qaeda, or for terrorists. And not only that, if your priest stood up at the beginning of Mass next Sunday and announced that he was offering Mass for Osama bin Laden, what sort of reaction do you think he would get?

The teachings of Jesus are as radical today as they were when they were first announced. They call us to a way of life that is both more challenging and more rewarding. Catholicism is not easy. It is an advanced way of life that requires all of our being; the Gospels are a constant reminder to us all of what we are created for and called to.

• Beyond the Gospels •

Once you have familiarized yourself with the Gospels, I would suggest that you then read the narrative books. Of the seventy-three books in the Bible, fourteen are narrative books:

Genesis
Exodus
Numbers
Joshua
Judges
1 Samuel
2 Samuel
1 Kings
2 Kings
Ezra
Nehemiah
1 Maccabees
Luke
Acts

By reading these narrative books in order you begin to see the big picture—the chronological story of God's relationship with humanity.

Begin by familiarizing yourself with the Gospels. Then read the fourteen narrative books in order to get a sense of the whole story. Finally, explore the other books of the Bible, keeping in mind the Gospels and the big picture revealed by the narrative books.

The Bible is the most influential book in history. Certainly, the Old Testament has special value for those of Jewish belief and both the Old and New Testaments have special significance to those of Christian belief. But even outside of the religious significance it is impossible to ignore the relevance and influence the Bible has had on human history. From historic and sociological perspectives it would seem to me impossible to ignore its value. Even from a purely secular point of view the Bible has enormous relevance, even when viewed solely from an academic perspective. But our modern secular culture seems intent on ignoring the most influential writings of all time. I am continually astounded at how many so-called educated people have not read the Bible.

• Stories, Questions, and Prayers •

Whether you are beginning your first quest to read the Bible or your next quest, as you do I would encourage you to pay attention to stories, questions, and prayers.

Stories. The Bible is the single story that has shaped and is shaping human history. At the same time, it is a collection of stories. We find that the greatest stories ever told are in the Bible, and every other story is only a variation of one of the biblical tales that echo throughout history. The reason they echo throughout history is because they are the stories of men and women as they struggle to know themselves, to know God, and to work out their salvation. In this way they are the stories of all men and women, and thus are ever fresh.

People are often shocked by the human weakness of key characters in biblical stories. Many are surprised, even scandalized, that God would use people with such monumental vices and shortcomings to reach out to humanity and give us hope for the future.

The danger is to read the Bible as an observer. It is easy to read these stories from the cold distance of an objective observer and not allow them to penetrate our lives. People have been doing just this ever since these stories were written. The challenge is to get involved.

It is all too easy to read the story of Moses leading the Israelites out of slavery and into the desert and think that we have nothing to learn, or that we would never complain like the Israelites did when food was scarce. The temptation is to read the Gospels and believe that we would never be cruel, calculating, vindictive, and hard-hearted, like some of the Pharisees were. We are tempted to presume that we would be the one leper who returns. But the ultimate temptation is to read the Bible and see ourselves only in Jesus.

Every single person in the Bible is put there to serve you. This procession of people, with their strengths and weaknesses, their faults, failings, flaws, talents, and abilities, their virtues and their vices, are your servants. Hidden between the lines of these ancient texts, they wait, wanting to teach you the great truths of the journey.

They provide this invaluable service by acting as mirrors. What do you see when you look into a mirror? Yes, yourself. These men and women afford you the opportunity to look deep into your divided heart and see your *self*—the good and the bad, that which is worthy and that which is in need of redemption. Until you have learned to see yourself in every person in the Scriptures, you have not read the Bible.

The stories that fill the Bible are the stories of hundreds of men and women and their struggles to walk with God, to make the journey of the soul, to surrender and allow God to save them. These are the stories of men and women who have tried and succeeded, or struggled and failed in their quest to become the-best-version-of-themselves. In some of these characters we find great success in this journey. In others we find great failure. But in most we find an intriguing mixture of both failure and success, the humanity that resonates with us deeply because it reminds us of our own struggles. Most draw near to God only to abandon his ways; then from the anguish of the brokenness and emptiness of their sin, they once again draw near to God and return to his ways.

There is perhaps no better example than Peter. One of the first to be gathered into Jesus' inner circle, Peter leaves everything behind to follow Jesus. Later, he turns his back on Jesus, denying he even knows him. But after Jesus' Resurrection, Peter becomes the unifying voice for the early Church.

Can you relate to Peter? Have you ever ignored what you knew in good conscience was the right thing to do because you were afraid what people might think of you?

As we discussed earlier, stories have a very powerful impact on our lives. They can transform civilizations. A story can win or lose a war. Stories can conquer the hearts of millions and transform enemies into friends. They can help heal the sick. The proud despise them because they are simple, but stories are one of the most powerful agents in history. They can reform the political or spiritual temperament of an age. Stories can be either light or darkness.

What stories are you allowing to direct your life?

Questions. We all have questions, and how we respond to them often determines the direction of our lives. In fact, the questions we ask of ourselves and of life are often more important than the answers we find. The reason is because if you ask the wrong questions you always get the wrong answers.

Our modern culture is asking all the wrong questions, and that is why so many are living lives of quiet desperation. These are the questions we are encouraged to ask by this so-called advanced culture: What do I want to do? What's in it for me? Will it feel good? How can I get people to serve me? How can I do less and get more? How can I get more power? What do I need to do to feel safe and secure? All of these questions lead us along the lonely path of self-centeredness. In this scenario, we place ourselves at the center of the universe. Do we really expect to find happiness by building our lives on such a distorted view of life and reality? We place ourselves at the center of human history, and by doing so isolate ourselves from any chance of lasting happiness.

As we read the Bible, we come across many people who fled from God's designs, but they never found happiness in their own plans. It was not until they turned back to God and said, "Here I am Lord, I come to do your will," (1 Samuel 3:4) that they experienced the wholeness and fulfillment they had been yearning for all along. Humanity's greatest foolishness is the discredited fantasy that we can find lasting happiness separate from the will of God.

The questions we ask are important—those we ask of ourselves, of our spouses, our children, our employees and employer, our friends, and the occasional pilgrim stranger who crosses our path.

Questions are an integral part of the spiritual journey. The temptation is to despise questions and the uncertainty they represent. But uncertainty is a spiritual gift designed to help us to grow. From time to time, great questions arise in our hearts and our minds. When that happens to you, don't let your heart be troubled. Learn to enjoy uncertainty. Learn to love the questions. The questions are life.

Three or four years ago, my brother Andrew gave me a copy of a book titled *Letters to a Young Poet*. It is a small book that contains a collection of letters written by the great German lyric poet Rainer Maria Rilke to Franz Kappus, who at the time was a young aspiring poet. In one of the letters, Rilke penned some words that have remained ingrained on my heart since I read and underlined them in that small volume: "Be patient toward all that is unresolved in your heart and try to love the questions themselves like locked rooms and like books that are written in a foreign tongue. Do not now seek the answers, which cannot be given you because you would not be able to live them. And the point is, to live everything. Live the questions now. Perhaps you will then gradually, without noticing it, live along some distant day into the answer."

Try to enjoy the wonder of the questions in your life. Allow your soul to breathe deeply, as the body must do sometimes to live among certain circumstances. Stand amid the uncertainty of the great questions life proposes, take a deep breath, and enjoy them.

The Bible is full of questions. Every person we experience in the Scriptures is asking a question, explicitly or implicitly, of life, of God, of themselves. As you pass from book to book, and story to story, be mindful of the questions each person is asking.

And if you happen upon God asking a question, pay close attention. God has no need to ask questions; he already has all the answers. So when he does ask a question, he asks not for his sake, but for ours. He asks questions like a great teacher: God asks questions to educate.

The perfect example of this divine questioning is in the third chapter of Genesis. God arrives in the garden at the time of the afternoon breeze as he does each day. Only on this particular day, Adam and Eve have hidden themselves. God calls out to them, "Where are you?" (Genesis 3:9) He doesn't ask because he doesn't know where they are. He asks because he wants them to realize where they are. God wants Adam and Eve to realize the absurdity of trying to hide from him. He wants them to be aware that they have turned their backs on him, gone against his life-giving designs, and rejected his friendship. By calling out to them, "Where are you?" he causes them to realize where they are and where they should be.

I often hear his call in the moments of the day in the very same way: I find myself wandering from the path, and he calls out to me, "Where are you?" I pray we can all learn to hear his gentle voice in the circumstances of our daily lives.

Prayers. Woven into these ageless stories and the great questions the Bible raises we also find some of the most beautiful prayers ever written.

The prayer of Jabez is just one example: "Oh, that you would truly bless me and enlarge my territory, that your hand might be with me, that you would keep me from evil, that I may cause no pain." (1 Chronicles 4:10) But this is just one example of the hundreds of prayers that emerge as we read the Bible.

When you are confused or troubled, weary or distracted, and finding it difficult to concentrate during prayer, use these prayers. I often use a Psalm as my last prayer of the day. I kneel beside my bed and just pray the words of the Psalm slowly. Sometimes I go through them one after another, day by day. At other times, at the end of a long day I just turn to one of my favorites in search of guidance or comfort.

The Bible is the richest treasury of prayers. Some of the prayers are obvious, like the Psalms, but others are treasures hidden among the stories, waiting to be discovered.

Amid the hustle and bustle of a busy day, I like to use what I call the First Christian Prayers to keep me in tune with my spiritual priorities. The First Christian Prayers is the name I have given to the words people spoke to Christ during his lifetime. When we pray, we speak and listen to God. These words were spoken directly to Jesus—true God and true man—so I believe they have a special power.

When I sense that God is calling me to something, but I'm not sure what, or when I have a decision to make and don't know which option to favor, I pray the words of the blind man: "Lord, open my eyes so that I may see." (Matthew 20:33) I pray them over and over in the moments of the day, using them as a mantra in the gaps between activities—at a stoplight, in line at the supermarket, when I am on hold on the telephone.

During times of doubt, questioning, or confusion, I use the prayer of the father of the possessed boy: "Lord I believe, help my unbelief." (Mark 9:24)

At other times I use the words of the criminal next to Jesus on the cross: "Jesus, remember me when you come into your Kingdom." (Luke 23:42)

And one of my very favorite prayers is the words of Peter when Jesus asks him three times, "Do you love me?" and Peter replies, "Lord, you know all things, you know that I love you." (John 21:17) Sometimes I use this prayer when I have offended God with my words or actions. At other times I use them when I feel hopeless or inadequate in my attempts to express my love for God.

When my sinfulness overwhelms me, I pray, "If you wish you can make me clean." (Matthew 8:2)

I pray these simple prayers over and over again throughout the day. They allow me to stay connected to God even among the many activities that can make my days very busy.

• 77 Years •

If you were born in 1900 your life expectancy was forty-seven years. Today the average American lives for seventy-seven years. This is my question for you: How are you going to tell God that you didn't have time to read his book?

The Bible is not just another book or collection of books. Words have value according to who writes them or speaks them. If a liar tells you something, you don't give his words any attention. But if an honest and honorable man tells you something, even if what he says challenges your deepest personal beliefs you will consider his words carefully, because you respect him as a man of integrity.

The Word of God deserves to be approached with reverence and awe. It is all too easy to think that we know a certain story, and to tune out as a result. But to do so would be a mistake. The Word of God is constantly new and fresh, even for those who have spent a lifetime exploring it. The reason is because our lives are constantly changing, we are constantly changing, and our relationships with God and others are constantly changing.

If you have not yet had a life-changing experience with the Bible, I am so excited for the opportunity that is before you at this time. My hope is that this chapter has intrigued you, and made you comfortable enough to pick up the Bible and begin a fabulous new adventure in your spiritual life.

Chapter Five

FASTING

In a world obsessed with pleasure the fifth pillar may demonstrate the relevance of our spirituality more than any of the other spiritual disciplines. You and I were created to love and be loved, and as such we yearn to love and be loved. As long as men and women have this yearning, the practices and traditions of our faith will be relevant. Let me explain.

It is often said that in our present age there is a poverty of love. Divorce rates are usually cited to support this claim. But I would like to suggest that our culture is not experiencing a poverty of love, but rather a poverty of self-possession. Our ability to love is directly linked to the level of self-possession that we have. In order to love, in order to put another before ourselves, we need self-possession. The person who has little self-possession thinks only of himself and constantly places his desires before the needs of others. The very act of loving is an act of self-donation, of giving ourselves to another. But in order to give ourselves, we must first possess ourselves. It is this self-possession that has been massively diminished by the hedonistic ideas of our culture. Broken relationships, soaring divorce rates, relationships that stay together only for convenience, and dysfunction within even the healthiest relationships are just the symptoms. The disease is our lack of self-possession.

All the spiritual disciplines that make up the incredible landscape of Catholic spirituality are designed in one way or another to restore our lost self-possession so that we can once again love God and neighbor, and be loved the way we were created to be loved.

• In Search of a Vision •

Our age is in search of an authentic vision of the human person. Are we just animals? Are we intelligent animals? Or are we children of God? Are we the result of evolution, a big bang, the loving hand of a creator—or some combination of these? Are we here to grasp as much pleasure as possible in our brief time or is there a higher calling and purpose to our lives? The way we live, love, work, vote, and participate in society is a direct result of the vision of the human person that we subscribe to.

Here in America we spent more than thirty billion dollars last year on diet products. That is more than we spent on books, and more than the gross domestic product (GDP) of at least fifty nations in the world. Now, it would seem to me that the only diet most of us need is a little bit of discipline. But we don't want any discipline. We want someone to get on the infomercial and tell us that if we take this little pill twice a day, every day, we can eat whatever we want, whenever we want. We want someone to tell us that if we buy this piece of exercise equipment and work out for twenty minutes twice a week we will look like a supermodel. We want someone to tell us, "You can be healthy and happy without discipline."

The truth is, you cannot be healthy and happy without discipline. In fact, if you want to measure the level of happiness in your life, just measure the level of discipline in your life. You will never have more happiness than you have discipline. The two are directly related to one another.

And this, of course, is where the great gulf appears between the Church and the culture. The message delivered with unrelenting enthusiasm by our culture is, "You can be happy without discipline. Do whatever you feel like doing and you will be happy!" While the Church says, "You cannot be happy without discipline. In fact, discipline is the path to happiness!" Both messages promise happiness and yet they could not be more diametrically opposed. So which is it that will actually lead to the happiness we yearn for and were created for?

The message the Church conveys is a tough one to deliver. At one time or another, we have all had the difficulty of delivering a message about the importance of discipline. And yet, the Church consistently delivers this message, because the Church is deeply rooted in an understanding of what is required for the human person to thrive and flourish. Don't miss this: The Church has a vision of wholeness and holiness for the human person, and everything the Church does should help her members to become more perfectly who God created them to be.

This vision of the human person is critical in our development as individuals, communities, nations, and an entire human family. The reason is because our position on everything else flows from this vision of the human person. Our position on health care, social security, education, human sexuality, the role of work, business and economics, and so many other things all flow from this primary vision we have about the purpose of man. The Church's message stands so counter to that of the present culture because the Church is driven by this incredible vision for the human person.

But when you ask, "What is the culture's vision for the human person?" the silence is deafening. The culture doesn't have a vision for the human person. So what drives today's culture? Consumption.

And if the culture doesn't have a vision for the human person, it certainly doesn't have a vision for the family. In fact, the culture would prefer that every family be broken, because a broken family needs two dishwashers, two lawn mowers, and two of almost everything else. And if the culture could break families up two, three, or four ways, it would prefer that.

The absence of any desire to help people become the-best-version-of-themselves and explore the potential of the human person in our culture is alarming on a level so profound that it is more than likely that most people will not realize it until it is too late.

But it doesn't have to be that way. Imagine a culture in which music and the arts celebrated the beauty of the human person and inspired people to explore all of their God-given potential. Imagine a culture in which lawmakers were less concerned with special interests and more concerned with creating a society that encouraged and actively helped people to become the-best-version-of-themselves. Imagine a culture in which all men, women, and children were educated not simply to perpetuate commerce, but in such a way as they came to understand who and what they are, who and what they are capable of becoming, and how they could use their talents and abilities to make a unique contribution.

It may seem far from where we are, but such a culture is possible.

• Body and Soul •

You are a delicate composition of body and soul. This is the essential makeup of the human person. Your body and soul are carefully linked by your will and intellect. In its present form, your body is temporal. One day it will die, be buried, and decay. Your soul, however, is eternal. The body and the soul are constantly vying for dominance—so which should steer the ship? Does it make sense for something that is temporal to lead something that is eternal? No. That which is eternal should lead and guide that which is temporal. But as much as that makes sense in the context of an intellectual discussion, you and I both know how easy it is to allow ourselves to be seduced by the things of this world.

There are many voices in our lives: the voices of family and friends, the voices of teachers and culture, and the voices of art and history. Of course, in the midst of all these voices, deep within you is the voice of conscience. All of these voices influence us at different times and to varying extents. But there is another voice that plays a powerful role in our lives—the voice of the body.

Your body has a voice, and it talks to you constantly. You wake up, and the body cries out, "feed me," so you eat. A couple of hours later the body cries out, "I'm thirsty," so you drink. Later the body cries out, "I'm tired," so you rest. Again the body cries out, "feed me," and you do. When it's time to exercise your body cries out, "I don't feel like it," so you don't. And at the end of the day, the body calls out, "I'm ready for bed," so you sleep. Whether we are aware of it or not, our body is ordering us around most of the day. The body is always crying out, feed me, sleep me, please me, pamper me, nourish me, wash me, relieve me, water me. . . .

But where is this voice leading us?

In the modern climate, most people's bodies are winning the battle for dominance between body and soul. In a sense, the body is like money—a great servant, but a horrible master. Fasting is one of the ingenious practices that the Church teaches us to ensure that the body does not become our master.

• The Death of Discipline •

We seem to want to avoid discipline at almost any cost. Far from seeing discipline as a friend in our quest to love and be loved, we treat discipline as a disease. The notion of freedom proclaimed by the modern world is anti-discipline. But true freedom cannot be separated from discipline.

The most obvious example of this paradox is in our cultural approach to dieting, mentioned earlier. For more than two decades the diet industry has been among the fastest-growing industries in any sector of the economy. Every day, more and more products stock the shelves, while infomercials cram the airwaves. These programs claim their products perform wonders, and yet, if you've been to the beach lately, you can see that for the billions of dollars we spend on such products, we are still growing more and more overweight as a culture with every passing year. But now it has gone from the bizarre to the absurd!

What is it that people are looking for in these diets and diet products? And why do so many people fail in their approach to dieting?

As I have observed it, people want a diet that will allow them to eat whatever they want, whenever they want, yet still allow them to look great, feel great, and lose that undesired extra weight. Basically what we are looking for is a miracle product that will remove the need for any discipline in our eating and exercise habits so that we can continue to indulge in the hedonistic ways that violate the-best-version-of-ourselves at every turn.

Diets don't fail because the program wasn't any good. They don't fail because the product wasn't any good. Diets fail because we lack the discipline to adopt a program of eating and exercise that nurtures and promotes our maximum physical potential as a human being.

Moderation is the only diet most people need, but we seem to lack the inner strength to choose what is good, true, and right for us. We want what is good for us, but we lack the strength of will to choose it. This problem is not new or unique to the modern world. Men and women of every age have experienced this same difficulty. And this is one of the reasons that for thousands of years men and women have been practicing a variety of spiritual exercises. One of the many benefits of these spiritual exercises is that they strengthen our will.

Fasting is a primary example of these spiritual exercises. Open your heart and your mind. Set aside your prejudices and rediscover the genius of fasting and how it can change your life.

• Fasting in the Scriptures •

For the Hebrew people, fasting was infrequent and was usually employed as a sign of repentance. The Torah requires only one day of fasting each year: Yom Kippur, the Day of Atonement. Four extra days of fasting were added to the Jewish tradition much later, to commemorate the events leading to the destruction of Jerusalem.

The Israelites fasted at Samuel's urging, as they put away the false gods Baal and Ashtoreth and returned to Yahweh (cf. 1 Samuel 7:2-6). The entire Israelite army employed fasting as part of its preparation for battle (cf. Judges 20:26 and 2 Chronicles 20:3–4). Daniel fasted as he prayed, asking God to grant him the ability to understand the Scriptures (cf. Daniel 9:3). At the urging of Jonah and to save the city of Nineveh, the King proclaimed a fast, calling on the people to abandon wrongdoing and violence (cf. Jonah 3:7–9).

In each of these cases, fasting was used to humbly seek out God's will. Over and over again, the Old Testament makes it abundantly clear that genuine fasting involves turning away from evil and turning back to God. Fasting that involves no such conversion of the heart is useless. Isaiah speaks out against fasting detached from conversion, announcing the worthlessness of fasting in the wrong spirit (cf. Isaiah 58:3–7). The Scriptures continually remind us that external actions are insufficient; they must be joined to some internal conversion of the heart.

The New Testament also highlights the ancient spiritual practice of fasting, and the life and teachings of Jesus provide particular insight into its roles and meaning.

Before Jesus began his public life, he was "led by the Spirit into the desert," where he fasted for forty days (Matthew 4:1). Jesus didn't fast in atonement for his sins; he was sinless. He fasted in preparation for his mission. And the fact that Jesus was led by the Spirit out into the desert to fast is perhaps the greatest evidence we have that fasting is not merely a physical practice or another personal accomplishment; rather, it is a spiritual exercise.

In the desert, Jesus was tempted by the devil to abandon his fasting and have his fill. Jesus rebuked him, saying, "Man does not live on bread alone, but on every word that comes from the mouth of God." (Matthew 4:4) Fasting is a sharp reminder that there are more important things in life than food. Authentic Christian fasting helps to release us from our attachments to the things of this world. It is often these worldly attachments that prevent us from becoming the-best-version-of-ourselves. Fasting also serves as a reminder that everything in this world is passing and thus encourages us to consider life beyond death.

Go without food for several hours and you quickly realize how truly weak, fragile, and dependent we are. This knowledge of self strips away arrogance and fosters a loving acknowledgment of our utter dependence on God.

Later during his public life, Jesus was challenged and questioned as to why his disciples didn't fast like the disciples of John the Baptist and the Pharisees. In his response, he revealed one of the prime purposes of fasting: "Can the wedding guests fast while the bridegroom is with them? As long as they have the bridegroom with them, they cannot fast. But the days will come when the bridegroom is taken away from them, and then they will fast on that day." (Mark 2:19–20)

One of the prime purposes of fasting is to help us become aware of God's presence in our lives and in the world around us. Fasting also makes us aware of God's absence in different areas of our lives. Since Jesus—God and man—was already in their presence, the disciples did not need to fast as we do while Jesus was with them.

Jesus instructed his disciples only once specifically concerning fasting. During the Sermon on the Mount in Matthew's Gospel, Jesus speaks of fasting in the same way he spoke of almsgiving and prayer. "When you fast, do not look gloomy like the hypocrites. They neglect their appearance, so that they may appear to others to be fasting. Amen, I say to you, they have received their reward. But when you fast, anoint your head and wash your face, so that you may not appear to be fasting, except to your Father who is hidden. And your Father who sees what is hidden will reward you." (Matthew 6:16–18)

As with prayer and almsgiving, Jesus calls us to remember that fasting is a spiritual exercise, and as such is primarily an action of the inner life. We do not fast to impress other people. We fast to cultivate the inner life. Fasting should be an occasion of joy, not a cause of sadness. Authentic fasting draws us nearer to God and opens our hearts to receive his many gifts.

There is one other occasion when Jesus mentions fasting. In my own life, this has been the most important passage relating to the great spiritual exercise of fasting. I believe this passage holds one of the greatest practical spiritual lessons, and yet, most modern Bibles have removed this passage or altered it.

In Mark's Gospel, we are told of a man who brings his possessed boy to Jesus for healing. The father of the boy explains that he brought the boy to Jesus' disciples, but they were unable to heal him even though they were able to heal many others with similar afflictions. When Jesus arrives at this scene, he rebukes the unclean spirit, ordering it to come out of the boy, and the child is cured. The disciples were confused about why they were not able to cast out the demon. So, when the crowd had dispersed and they were alone with Jesus, "his disciples asked him in private, 'Why was it that we could not cast it out?' And he told them, 'This kind of spirit can only be cast out through prayer and fasting.'" (Mark 9:28–29)

You may believe that people do not suffer from possession by demons in our modern age. Don't be so sure. The demons of our modern age are in some cases subtler than the demons of Jesus' time. I assure you that many drunks take on the qualities of a person possessed by a demon, and there are many other types of possession that have become frighteningly common today. Next time someone loses his temper, ask yourself if he resembles someone possessed. Look around and I think you will discover that you quite often cross paths with people who are possessed in one way or another by "evil spirits."

In my own life, I have known the demon of habitual sin. When I first turned to God in my late teen years, I was possessed by such a demon. I tried with all my might to wrestle with it, but nothing worked. I prayed, begging God to free me from this sin, but he didn't. I employed all the power of my will, but that didn't work either. Then one day I noticed the previous passage in Mark's Gospel and at that moment I felt the hand of God upon my shoulder. Encouraged by the example of a friend, several weeks later I began to fast each Friday, eating only bread and drinking only water. I offered this fasting to God, asking him to liberate me, and it was then that God cast the demon of habitual sin from my life. I believe with my whole being that some demons in our lives "can only be cast out through prayer and fasting." (Mark 9:29) If you are suffering under the slavery of ingrained bad habits, turn to God through prayer and fasting. If you are being tormented by the demons of habitual sin, turn to God through prayer and fasting.

It is important to note how different the reasons for fasting are from the reasons for dieting. Fasting is by its very nature a statement of humility, while dieting is usually linked to ego, vanity, and pride. It is also interesting to realize that the secular culture takes all things sacred and waters them down, ridicules them by adopting the opposite extreme, or separates them from their true meaning and purpose. Dieting is the secularization of the great spiritual exercise of fasting. But dieting is devoid of the strongest motives and reasons: repentance, self-denial, humility, self-mastery, and the spiritual power that comes from these dispositions.

You are a delicate composition of body and soul. Fasting is to the body what prayer is to the soul. Indeed, fasting is the prayer of the body, and bodily fasting leads to spiritual feasting.

• The History of Christian Fasting •

After the death, Resurrection, and ascension of Jesus, fasting quickly became an integral part of early Christian practice. At that time, several Jewish groups were fasting on Tuesdays and Thursdays. To distinguish their own practice, the first Christians fasted on Wednesdays and Fridays. In the Judeo-Christian world, a fast day generally implied abstaining from food until the evening meal, which would be served after sundown.

While some people argue that fasting was not introduced into the Christian way of life for centuries, there is considerable evidence that this is not the case. In fact, fasting was a part of the earliest Christians' way of life. A very early manuscript known as *The Didache,* which outlines Christian practice and belief, recommends to Christians, "fast for those who persecute you."

Fasting was also common among these early Christian communities in preparation for the sacraments, including the Eucharistic meal and baptism. In the case of adult baptism, both the baptizer and the one to be baptized would observe a fast in preparation.

In the fourth century, the Church began to regulate the practice of fasting, and since then, the practice has changed considerably at different junctures. In the Middle Ages, distinctions began to emerge regarding the amount and kind of food to be taken on a fast day. It was at this time that it became a rule to abstain from meat, eggs, and dairy products on fast days.

The number of fast days gradually increased over the years, as the eves of major feast days and the ember days were designated as fast days. And while the number of fast days was increasing, dispensations were being granted for a growing number of reasons. All this conspired to make the whole practice of fasting more and more complex. These growing complexities tended to transform the practice into more of a legal matter than a spiritual practice, and moved the focus from inner transformation to outward display. The motive for fasting began to shift toward obligation and away from conversion and penance.

While there have been many changes in the practice of fasting over the centuries, the Church's understanding of it has remained consistent. The great thirteenth-century scholar, saint, and doctor of the Church, Thomas Aquinas, wrote of these three values of fasting: for the repression of one's concupiscence (strong desires) of the flesh, for the atonement for one's sins, and to better dispose oneself to higher things.

It was perhaps in the monasteries that the purpose and goals of fasting were preserved throughout the ages. Here it remained clear that that primary goal and purpose was union with God. It is this point that has been grossly underemphasized. This was largely due to the erroneous view that union with God was a reward reserved only for a few saints and mystics.

In the modern age, we have also seen many changes in the practice of fasting. Prior to 1917, Catholics were required to fast throughout Lent except on Sundays, taking only one meal per day. We were also expected to abstain from meat, eggs, and dairy products on all prescribed fast days, as well as every Friday and Saturday. By the early 1950s, fast days for Catholics in the United States consisted of one main meal and two small meatless meals.

In 1966, Pope Paul VI warned of the dangers of a legalistic approach to fasting and offered some new direction for the practice of fasting in the modern era in his Apostolic Constitution on Penance. He reminded Catholics that the outward expression of fasting should always be accompanied by the inner attitude of conversion. In this document, Paul VI not only stressed the value of fasting and other forms of penitence but also reminded Catholics everywhere of the importance the early Christians placed on linking the external act of fasting with inner conversion, prayer, and works of charity. In doing so, Paul VI echoed Saint Augustine's idea: "Do you wish your prayer to fly toward God? Give it two wings: fasting and almsgiving." Having reasserted the value of fasting among prayer and charity as the "fundamental means of complying with the divine precepts of penitence," Paul VI then simplified the regulations for fasting and abstinence and handed authority over to local bishops' conferences to establish guidelines according to their culture.

Here in the America, the United States Conference of Catholic Bishops issued a pastoral statement later that same year announcing, "Catholics in the United States are obliged to abstain from the eating of meat on Ash Wednesday and on all Fridays during the season of Lent. They are also obliged to fast on Ash Wednesday and Good Friday." The pastoral statement encouraged the faithful to continue the traditional practice of Friday abstinence and also urged Catholics to perform works of charity in the spirit of penance, including visiting the sick and imprisoned, caring for the indigent, and giving alms to those in need. At the time, this was a radical shift that eliminated many of the old rules and regulations regarding fasting, abstinence, and penance. As a result, many Catholics felt they were no longer obliged to follow any specific penitential practices. Only a few were able to see the wisdom of the changes and realize that they were being called to a deeper spirit of penitential conversion.

Despite the fact that many modern Catholics have abandoned penance and particularly fasting, at every level the Church continues to affirm the great value of these practices as means for authentic spiritual growth. Throughout this modern era, popes and bishops have invited Catholics to fast and abstain, to pray and perform charitable works as time-tested ways of turning our attention toward God and the needs of our brothers and sisters. But amid the abundance and great wealth of advanced modern nations such as the United States, it is all too easy to be seduced into the self-absorbed lifestyles promoted by today's popular culture.

Today, fasting is more popular in secular circles than it is among Catholics. Health enthusiasts are turning to periodic fasting for cures to everything from insomnia to cancer. Others are adopting this ancient spiritual practice to "cleanse" the body of impurities such as oxidants and the excess chemicals used to fertilize our foods. Fasting has even found a place in many diet programs as a tool to achieve dramatic weight loss and proper weight maintenance.

I pray we can rediscover the value of this ancient spiritual practice as modern Catholics—not for God's sake, but for our own. I am utterly convinced that if we are to develop the inner freedom to resist the temptations that face us in the modern world, we must learn to assert the dominance of the spirit over the body, of the eternal over the temporal. If the spirit within each of us is to reign, then the body must first be tamed. Prayer won't achieve this, works of charity won't achieve this, and power of the will won't achieve it. This is a task for fasting, abstinence, and other acts of penance.

• Lenten Fasting •

There is great wisdom in the Christian practice of fasting. Though Christian fasting has been largely abandoned, the one expression of fasting (and penitential practice) that seems to have survived the turmoil of this modern era is that of Lenten penance. Although I suspect it is hanging on by a very thin cultural thread, which will break unless we can make people aware of the great beauty and spiritual significance of these acts.

As I have said over and over again in my books and talks, our lives change when our habits change. The Lenten experience is a perfect example of the Church's intimate understanding of the nature of the human person. The forty days of Lent are an ideal period for renewal. Lent is the perfect span of time to form new life-giving habits and abandon old self-destructive habits. But most of us just give up chocolate and when Easter arrives we are not much further advanced spiritually than we were at the beginning of Lent.

• Fasting and You •

Our faith seeks to integrate the relationship between body and soul. There is a war taking place within you. It is the constant battle between your body and your soul. At every moment of the day, both are vying for dominance. If you wish to have a rich and abundant experience of life, you must allow your soul to soar. But in order to do that, you first need to tame and train the body. You cannot win this war once a week, once a year, or even once a day. From moment to moment, our desires need be harnessed.

Fasting should be a part of our everyday spirituality. For example, suppose you have a craving for a Coke, but you have cranberry juice or a glass of water instead. It is the smallest thing. Nobody notices. And yet, by this simple action you say no to the cravings of the body that seek to control you and assert the dominance of the soul. The will is strengthened and the soul is a little freer. In that one action you create an ounce of self-possession.

Or, say your soup tastes a little dull. You could add salt and pepper, but you don't. It's a little thing. It's nothing. But if it's done for the right reasons, with the correct inner attitude, it is a spiritual exercise. You say no to the body. In doing so, you assert the dominance of the spirit. The will is strengthened and the soul is a little freer. Again, you create an ounce of self-possession.

Never leave a meal table without practicing some form of fasting. It is these tiny acts that harness the body as a worthy servant and strengthen the will for the great moments of decision that are a part of each of our lives.

Beyond these small moments of fasting, we should each seek more intense encounters with fasting and abstinence if we are serious about the spiritual life—not because it is in the catechism, but because it will help us to turn away from sin and turn back to God, which is why it is in the catechism. Fasting helps us to turn our backs on the-lesser-version-of-ourselves and embrace the-best-version-of-ourselves.

Perhaps you can fast one day a week—two small meals, one full meal, and nothing to eat between meals. Perhaps you can fast one day a week on bread and water. Or maybe all you can manage at this time is to give up coffee for a day. Maybe you can't even give up coffee for the whole day, maybe just for two hours. Personalize your fasting. You know what it is that has a grip on you. Friday has always been a traditional day of fasting, and I would encourage you to employ this tradition in your own way. Only you can decide what the right fast is for you.

Try not to be prideful about it. Come humbly to God in prayer, and there in the classroom of silence, decide upon some regular practice of fasting and abstinence. Then, from time to time, review this practice. If you feel called to add to it, add to it.

It is also important to recognize that not all forms of fasting involve food. You can fast from judging others, criticizing, cursing, or complaining, to name but a few.

Two powerful forms of fasting that helped me to grow tremendously were the practice of silence and of stillness. From time to time, fast from noise and movement. Sit perfectly still in silence for twenty minutes. It isn't easy. This is perhaps why so many people never seriously adopt the habit of prayer. After you have become comfortable in the silence, be still for twenty minutes. Be completely still. It is difficult. Yet I am convinced that silence and stillness are two of the greatest spiritual tools.

Fasting is a simple yet powerful way to turn toward God. If there is a question in your life, fast and ask God to lead you. He will. If you have a persistent sin that you just cannot seem to overcome, then fast. Some demons can only be cast out by prayer and fasting together.

Fasting is radically countercultural, but so is Christianity.

• The Universe and You •

Until this point, I have avoided discussing the idea of fasting as a form of penance to reverse the effect of sin. I have done this because there is such a negative stigma that goes with this idea in our modern world. But I would be remiss not to discuss it and try to shed some positive light on this idea.

Even before kindergarten, we are taught the governing laws of the universe. One of these is the law of cause and effect: Every cause has an effect; every action has a reaction.

In a sense, the universe has a perfect accounting system. This is just one tiny aspect of the wonder and perfection of God's creation. These laws are designed to help keep everything in balance and harmony. As a result, no debt in the universe goes unpaid. All debts must be settled.

This is where the link between penance and fasting emerges. I repeat, sooner or later, all debts must be repaid.

We practice fasting as a form of penance not because we want to punish ourselves or destroy ourselves, but rather to express sorrow for our moral failings and to be restored to wholeness. The Church invites us to the spiritual practice of fasting not because she wants us to feel guilty or have a poor self-image, but rather so we can be liberated. In the process we are given grace to strive with ever more determination to become the-best-version-of-ourselves.

It goes without saying that if you sit on the couch every day for ten years eating potato chips and drinking beer, the effects of those actions will be increased weight and poor health. In order to erase the weight gained and return to optimum health, you would need to exercise and focus on eating foods that fuel the body with nourishment and energy. Neither of these is enjoyable at first, but they erase the effects of poor past actions that led you to become less than the-best-version-of-yourself.

The same is true spiritually. Every time we sin, it has an impact on our souls. Every word, thought, or action that betrays the-best-version-of-yourself also damages your relationship with God and neighbor. You can't see it, but it's there. When you sin, you not only damage your soul but you also increase your *tendency toward sin* and your *appetite for sin* in the future.

It is true that God forgives our sins through the Sacrament of Reconciliation, but if the effects these sins have on our character and soul are to be reversed, some form of penance will be required. Fasting is one spiritual practice that can help restore the soul to its intended beauty, reduce our tendency toward those actions that are self-destructive and sinful, and reduce our appetite for sin in the future.

• Always a Means, Never an End •

Fasting is a means, but never an end. The purpose of fasting is to assist the soul in turning back to God. The benefits of fasting are innumerable, but all these benefits are secondary to the desire to embrace God more fully in our lives.

Whatever form of fasting you decide to employ in your life, you will have good days and bad days. You will have successes and failures. Stick to it. Don't give up. If you fail, try again.

I was back in Australia at the beginning of Lent several years ago. On Ash Wednesday evening, the phone rang as I was walking past it, so I answered it. "Is that you, Uncle Matt?" a little voice said. It was my niece Zoe.

"How are you, Zoe?" I asked.

"I'm good, Uncle Matt."

"What did you do today?" I inquired.

"Oh . . . it was a busy day. I went to school, then I went to volleyball practice, then I came home and did my homework, and then we went to church and I got ashes."

"What did Father talk about at church?" I asked.

"He talked about giving up things for Lent. Guess what I'm giving up, Uncle Matt," she said.

"I don't know, what are you giving up this year, Zoe?"

"I'm giving up Coca-Cola."

"But Zoe, you really like Coca-Cola."

"I know, but Father talked about giving up something that will be really hard. So I'm giving up Coke."

Two days later, on Friday evening, I was at a basketball game with my two nieces, Emma and her sister, Zoe. Emma is the elder and she was about fourteen at the time; Zoe was twelve. Emma was playing in the basketball game, and Zoe was sitting next to me with five or six of her giggling little friends from school.

About half way through of the game, I looked over and Zoe was guzzling down a large bottle of Coke. I didn't say anything. I just smiled to myself and turned back to the game. But about five minutes later, I felt a tug on my shirt and a tap on my shoulder.

"Uncle Matt, I forgot."

"You forgot what, Zoe?" I asked.

"Oh, Uncle Matt, I forgot I gave up Coke for Lent and I just drank a bottle of Coke." I didn't say anything. I just looked at her and smiled. She sighed and said, "Oh well. It's all over now. I'll have to wait till next year."

Our lives change when our habits change. Our habits change when we make resolutions, remind ourselves of those resolutions, hold ourselves accountable for them, and perform them. Sometimes we fail, but there is no success that isn't checkered with failure. Don't give up. Press on, little by little.

The spiritual journey is not made a mile at a time. More often than not, the advances in the journey are too small even to measure. But they all add up to a lifetime of joy-filled challenges and an eternity in union with God and everything that is good, true, beautiful, and noble.

Our bodies are vehicles that God has given our souls to experience life in the material realm. Until we get a grip on our bodies, we will never get a grip on life. Until we learn to reign over our bodies we never really experience all that life can be.

Chapter Six

SPIRITUAL READING

Books change our lives. Most people can identify a book that has marked a life-changing period for them. It was probably a book that said just the right thing at just the right time. They may have been just words on a page, but they came to life for you and in you, and because of them you will never again be the same. Books really do change our lives, because what we read today walks and talks with us tomorrow.

Earlier, in our discussion of prayer and contemplation, we spoke of the cause-and-effect relationship between thought and action. Thought determines action, and one of the most powerful influences on thought is the material we choose to read.

Reading is to the mind what exercise is to the body and prayer is to the soul.

• An Ancient Tradition •

Spiritual reading is an ancient tradition. It existed in the Church long before we had books to read, when every manuscript had to be copied by hand because the printing press had not yet been invented. In those days, this spiritual tradition was mostly confined to the monasteries, where the monks had access to manuscripts of the Scriptures and other great spiritual writings.

The goal of spiritual reading is to ignite the soul with a desire to grow in virtue and thus become the-best-version-of-oneself. Like all other spiritual exercises and activities, spiritual reading seeks to encourage us to live a life of holiness.

• What Should We Read? •

Reading of the Scriptures, especially the New Testament and in particular the four Gospels, obviously holds first place on our spiritual reading list. It has been my experience that all men and women of good will take delight in the Gospels as they become familiar with them. They are the best education of the life and teachings of Jesus Christ. Nothing ignites the soul to imitate the Divine Master more than an intimate familiarity with the story of his life, work, and teachings.

The Old Testament can also be very valuable as a source of spiritual reading, though in this case some books are harder to draw nourishment from than others. In books such as Psalms and Proverbs, our hearts are easily stirred to live a better life and to strive for virtue through our relationships with God, neighbor, and self. On the other hand, many of the historical and prophetic books require some rather serious preparation if we are to understand the culture and context in which they were written and their intended message.

Beyond the Scriptures, there are also a great many spiritual writers who can be of assistance to us in our adventure of salvation. These masters and mentors of the spiritual life are always available for consultation.

The great masters of spiritual writing are able to set aside the issues of the day and their own personal agendas, and place at the center of their writing God's dream for us to grow each day in virtue and holiness. In their writings, you will always hear a call to become a better person. As you read their words, you will constantly feel inspired and challenged to change, grow, and to become the-best-version-of-yourself.

They are also very worthy mentors, and if you allow them into your life, they will reveal your defects for you with great discretion and kindness. They point out your weaknesses not to belittle you, but so that you might grow and become all you are capable of being. They do this by holding a spiritual mirror before you and calling you to self-examination. They then encourage you to make generous resolutions. They lead you into divine cooperation with the Holy Spirit. They will also teach you how to maximize the impact and influence of your strengths.

It is within these bounds that the classical definition of spiritual reading has been confined until now. But for the sake of the modern Catholic who finds him- or herself in the midst of the information age, I would like to stretch those boundaries a little, while at the same time keeping our sight firmly fixed on the goal of this ancient practice.

I believe there is also a place within the context of spiritual reading for us to study certain issues, and that most former Catholics, non-practicing Catholics, and many disengaged Catholics are separated from the Church over one issue. It may be a different issue for each person, but there is usually one issue that sparks the separation and leads people to turn their backs on the Church. For some the issue is contraception, for others it is abortion, and for many modern Catholics it is divorce. I suspect that the great majority of non-practicing Catholics are not joining us each Sunday because of a very limited number of issues, perhaps five or six at the most. With that in mind, we have a duty to study and know those issues so we can build the necessary bridges of truth and knowledge that will allow them to return to the fullness of our ancient and beautiful faith.

If you want to grow in faith, identify the teaching of the Catholic Church that you find most difficult to understand and accept, then read about it. Study that issue. Get yourself a catechism and read what it says, but then look up the source texts, find other books that explain why the Church teaches what it teaches about that issue, and get to the heart of the matter. Don't read books by bitter authors who seek to tear the Church down. Read books by men and women of prayer who seek by their writing to reveal the truth and depth of the Church's teachings. If you approach that issue humbly the wisdom and beauty of Catholicism will be unveiled before your very eyes. The issues are so few; let's begin to study them.

• When, Where, and for How Long? •

When I first began to take the spiritual life seriously, I was very fortunate that my path crossed with that of a very holy priest. He was a man of prayer who was striving to grow in virtue and clearly focused on trying to live a holy life. His only concern in any of my conversations with him was my spiritual growth. He would say to me, over and over again, "God is calling you to a life of holiness." In the context of Confession, he would remind me that God calls us all to holiness. In our conversations about my struggles with prayer, he reminded me that I was called to holiness. When I asked his advice on situations in my personal life, and later in my business or ministry, he always reminded me that our number one concern must be to honor God's call to holiness in our lives and the lives of the people who cross our paths.

I say all this because he also used to suggest books for me to read. In each of them, I found worthy guides, spiritual masters, and grace-filled mentors who reinforced this teaching that God calls us all to become the-best-version-of-ourselves. God invites us to holiness.

Perhaps we find the litmus test of a good book right there: Is this book inviting me to live a life of holiness?

"Fifteen minutes a day," this old priest would say to me. "It's amazing how powerfully fifteen minutes with the right book can stir your soul." In the morning, in the evening, at lunchtime, whenever you can, find fifteen minutes each day to nourish yourself spiritually and intellectually with a good book. Try to do it at the same time every day. Perhaps it is before you go to work. Maybe it is in bed late at night. Then again, perhaps it is while you are eating your lunch. Find a quiet corner at work or at home and read. If you're not sure what to read, visit DynamicCatholic.com and request a list of ten books that changed my life.

You don't need two hours of reading every day, just fifteen minutes. But do it every day. Embrace spiritual reading as a daily discipline. Make it a part of your lifestyle. Remember, Catholicism is not a set of lifeless rules and regulations; Catholicism is a lifestyle. Start to build that lifestyle. Read for fifteen minutes every day, and it will become a habit—and our lives change when our habits change.

• Adult Education •

One of the challenges that is staring the Church in the face is the great need for adult education. Several generations have now managed to pass through the Catholic education system with little more than an elementary understanding of Catholicism. Over this time, more and more Catholics have decided not to send their children to Catholic schools or religious education programs. All this is having a devastating effect on future generations.

We could dream up all types of elaborate adult education programs, but my proposal is that we encourage Catholic adults to read good spiritual books. We cannot make up for lost ground overnight, but fifteen minutes a day is as good as any place to start.

My proposal will no doubt be overlooked by most, and frowned upon by others, because of its sheer simplicity. Nonetheless, let me assure you the simplest solution is usually the best, and hidden in our ancient traditions we will find the solutions to most of our modern problems.

Spiritual reading is a perfect example of an ancient solution to a modern problem. If every Catholic were to read a good Catholic book for fifteen minutes a day this habit alone could be a game changer for the Church in our times.

What percentage of Catholics do you think have read a Catholic book in the past twelve months? This is a question I have been posing to audiences of late. The consensus seems to be about one percent.

Now imagine for a moment what would happen if every Catholic in your parish read a good spiritual book for fifteen minutes a day. How would your parish change? If every Catholic spent fifteen minutes a day, every day, learning about his or her faith, how different would our Church be in a year? Five years? Ten years?

Rome wasn't built in a day. Most great things are achieved little by little.

• Keeping the Star in Sight •

Spiritual reading is a great tool to help us keep the great spiritual North Star in sight. When we view everything in relation to our call to become the-best-version-of-ourselves, everything finds meaning. Even the smallest and most menial tasks take on new life, for we come to understand that every action is a character-building action, for better or for worse.

Direct all your thoughts and actions toward the great spiritual North Star. What I mean is, find ways of spending time with your friends that help you all become the-best-version-of-yourselves. Similarly, find activities you can do as a family that draw the best out of each of you and challenge you to grow. In the same way, read books that make you want to become a better person, books that show you how to become the-best-version-of-yourself. Cast off the whimsical modern reading materials. What is in those magazines that will help you live a richer, fuller life? When was the last time you read a newspaper and said to yourself, "I'm a better person for having read that newspaper?" We have bought into the modern myth that we have to be up on everyone else's business.

Books change our lives. If you really want your life to change, read some good spiritual books. If you approach these books with a spirit of faith, a desire to grow in holiness, and a sincere intention to practice what you read, spiritual reading will become a powerful tool in your life.

Chapter Seven

THE ROSARY

Jim Castle was tired when he boarded his flight one night in Cincinnati. The forty-five-year-old management consultant had put on a weeklong series of business meetings and seminars, and now he sank gratefully into his seat, ready for the flight home to Kansas City.

As more passengers boarded, the plane hummed with conversation, mixed with the sound of bags being stowed. Then, suddenly, people fell silent. The quiet moved slowly up the aisle like an invisible wake behind a boat. Jim craned his neck to see what was happening and his mouth dropped open.

Walking up the aisle were two nuns clad in simple white habits with blue borders. He immediately recognized the familiar face, wrinkled skin, and warm eyes of one of the nuns. This was the face he'd seen so often on television and on the cover of *Time*. The two nuns halted, and Jim realized that his seat companion was going to be Mother Teresa.

As the last few passengers settled in, Mother Teresa and her companion pulled out rosaries. Jim noticed that each decade of the beads was a different color. The decades represented various areas of the world, Mother Teresa told him later, adding, "I pray for the poor and dying on each continent."

The airplane taxied to the runway, and the two women began to pray, their voices in a low murmur. Though Jim considered himself a not very engaged Catholic who went to church mostly out of habit, inexplicably he found himself joining in. By the time they whispered the final prayer, the plane had reached cruising altitude.

Mother Teresa turned toward him. For the first time in his life, Jim understood what people meant when they spoke of a person possessing an aura. As she gazed at him, a sense of peace filled him; he could see it no more than he could see the wind, but he felt it, just as surely as he felt a warm summer breeze. "Young man," she inquired, "do you pray the rosary often?"

"No, not really," he admitted.

She took his hand, and her eyes probed his. Then she smiled. "Well, you will now," and she dropped her rosary into his palm.

An hour later, Jim entered the Kansas City Airport, where he was met by his wife, Ruth. "What in the world?" Ruth asked when she noticed the rosary in his hand.

They kissed and Jim described the encounter. Driving home, he said, "I feel as if I met God's daughter."

Nine months later, Jim and Ruth visited Connie, a longtime friend of theirs. Connie told them she had ovarian cancer. "The doctor says it's a tough case," said Connie, "but I'm going to fight it. I won't give up."

Jim clasped her hand. Then, after reaching into his pocket, he gently twined Mother Teresa's rosary around her fingers. He told her the story and said, "Keep it with you, Connie. It may help."

Although Connie wasn't Catholic, her hand closed willingly around the small plastic beads. "Thank you," she whispered. "I hope I can return it."

More than a year passed before Jim saw Connie again. This time, face glowing, she hurried toward him and handed him the rosary. "I carried it all year," she said. "I've had surgery and have been having chemotherapy, too. Last month, the doctors did a second-look surgery, and the tumor's gone. Completely!" Her eyes met Jim's. "I knew it was time to give the rosary back."

The following fall, Ruth's sister Liz fell into a deep depression after her divorce. She asked Jim if she could borrow the rosary, and when he sent it, she hung it over her bedpost in a small velvet bag.

"At night I held on to it, just physically held on. I was so lonely and afraid," she said, "yet when I gripped that rosary, I felt as if I held a loving hand." Gradually, Liz pulled out of her depression and found a new perspective on life, and mailed the rosary back. "Someone else may need it," read the note that accompanied it.

Then one night a year or so later, a stranger telephoned Ruth. She'd heard about the rosary from a neighbor and asked if she could borrow it to take to the hospital where her mother lay in a coma. The family hoped the rosary might help their mother die peacefully.

A few days later, the woman returned the beads. "The nurses told me a coma patient can still hear," she said, "so I explained to my mother that I had Mother Teresa's rosary and that when I gave it to her she could let go; it would be all right. Then I put the rosary in her hand. Within minutes, we saw her face relax! The lines smoothed out until she looked so peaceful, so young." The woman's voice caught. "A few minutes later, she was gone." She gripped Ruth's hands, looked deep into her eyes, and said, "Thank you."

Is there special power in those humble beads? Or is the power of the human spirit simply renewed in each person who borrows the rosary? Jim only knows that requests continue to come, often unexpectedly. He always responds, though whenever he lends the rosary, he says, "When you're through needing it, send it back. Someone else may need it."

Jim's life has also changed since his unexpected meeting on the airplane. When he realized Mother Teresa carries everything she owns in a small bag, he made an effort to simplify his own life. He says, "I try to remember what really counts—not money, or titles, or possessions, but the way we love others."

• Why Have We Abandoned the Rosary? •

There are perhaps many reasons why modern Catholics have abandoned the rosary. One reason, no doubt, is the overemphasis some people have placed on the role of Mary and the rosary. But I very much doubt that this is the whole reason that Catholics en masse have stopped praying the rosary and teaching their children to pray the rosary in their homes and schools. The solution to the distortion or overemphasis of a good is never to abolish the good in question. The rosary deserves a place in our lives.

I suspect one of the reasons the rosary has become so unpopular during this modern era is because it is stereotypically considered the prayer of an overly pious old woman with little education and too much time on her hands. In a world where we bow to knowledge and academic degrees, piety is considered to border on superstition. But in truth, piety is reverence for God and devotion to God. Isn't part of the goal of every Christian life to devote oneself to God?

Catholics have abandoned the rosary today because we have been seduced by complexity. We give our allegiance and respect to complexity, but simplicity is the key to perfection. Peace in our hearts is born from simplicity in our lives. All the great leaders throughout history have agreed that usually the simplest solution is the best solution. The genius of God is simplicity. If you wish to tap into the wonder and glory of God, apply simplicity to your life and to your prayer.

Our lives are suffering under the intolerable weight of ever-increasing complexities. We complicate everything. And as this diseased fascination with complexity has swept across modern culture, it has also affected the way we approach prayer. Subsequently, as modern Catholics, we have deemed the rosary worthless. Don't despise simplicity. There is real power in it.

The rosary is not a prayer just for gray-headed old ladies with too much time on their hands. It is a rich practice of prayer that we can all benefit from.

Perhaps your objection is that you were forced to pray the rosary as a child. If this is the case, move beyond that experience and discover this beautiful prayer anew for yourself. Don't let your past rob you of your future.

• Benefits •

Contrary to what most people think, the first book I ever published was titled *Prayer & the Rosary*. Now, the fact that someone publishes a book about the rosary at the age of nineteen probably leads most people to assume that I grew up in one of those homes where the rosary was prayed together every night. I didn't. In fact, I have never prayed the rosary with my family—not even once.

So how did I come to have such a high regard for this simple prayer, which has been so ardently rejected by our sophisticated modern world? Let me tell you.

When I was in fourth grade, Mrs. Rutter taught us how to pray the rosary and gave us each a pair of rosary beads. I didn't pay much attention and I wasn't very interested, but for some reason I kept the beads in a place with my childhood treasures.

In fifth grade, Mr. Greck spoke a lot about Lourdes. His son had been miraculously cured there and every Friday he would lead the rosary in the chapel at lunchtime. If you got detention, you had to go to the rosary. I got detention occasionally, but the compulsory rosary didn't do much for my love of this prayerful devotion.

At sixteen, I met a man who was to become very instrumental in my spiritual journey. He was teaching a study-skills course that I was attending after school, and invited me one Saturday to visit a local nursing home. We walked to the nursing home and spoke about a lot of things, mostly about me, my sports, my part-time job, my aspirations in life, and my girlfriend. The experience that afternoon was the first of many encounters at nursing homes in my area that would begin to awaken my moral senses. As we walked home that day, he asked me if I would like to pray the rosary. I agreed. I mean, what else can you do in a situation like that? But for some reason, the prayers soothed me, and I began to pray the rosary on my own in the days and weeks ahead. Not long after that, I began to pray the rosary regularly with my good friend Luke.

I began praying the rosary because it is a form of prayer that I find very soothing, both mentally and spiritually. Today, I pray the rosary because I believe it is the simplest way to reflect upon the life and teachings of Jesus Christ. To place this in the context of our spiritual journey, I believe that as Christians we are called to imitate Jesus. It is impossible to imitate someone you do not know. We come to know him in the Scriptures, in the Sacraments, and through so many different people and places. The rosary is one other way. By praying the rosary, we can ponder many aspects of Jesus and his life in a relatively brief period of time. And, as we discussed earlier, the actions of our lives are determined by our most dominant thoughts. If our actions are to be like those of Christ then it helps to ponder his life and teachings regularly.

We spoke earlier about the power of stories. There is no more powerful story than that of Jesus Christ. This is the story that has formed and focused human history, and it is essential to our mission as Christians that we are intimately familiar with it. The rosary helps us to know his story and teaches us to integrate it into our own lives.

• Growth in Virtue •

One of the practical spiritual benefits of the rosary is its ability to help us grow in virtue. As I have studied the great spiritual masters of our Catholic tradition, I have discovered how essential virtue is to our journeys. When we connect the good and noble external acts of our lives with positive internal attitudes and intentions, we grow in virtue. As we begin to practice a virtue intentionally, it develops into a habitual virtue. But I have also learned that when you intentionally focus your energies toward growing in a particular virtue, you automatically grow in every other virtue. Virtue begets virtue. Eventually, the habitual effort to practice a virtue blossoms into spontaneous right action. I have found the rosary particularly helpful in my attempts to increase the practice of various virtues in my life.

The fruit of all spiritual exercises is an increase in the supernatural virtues: faith, hope, and love. Saint Paul speaks of them in his first letter to the Corinthians: "So faith, hope, and love remain, these three; but the greatest of these is love." (1 Corinthians 13:13) At a time when the world is so filled with doubt and skepticism, the beauty of faith shines forth. With so many people's hearts and minds suffering with depression, despair, and hopelessness, the splendor of hope is radiant. In a culture that exults the selfish attainment of pleasure and possessions, one eternal truth remains clear to all: Love is the only way.

Beyond the supernatural virtues, each decade of the rosary introduces practical examples of human virtues, and teaches us to practice these virtues in our own lives. Let's explore those human virtues now, one decade at a time.

• Twenty Lessons •

The actions of your life are determined by your most dominant thoughts. So turn your mind to those things that are good, true, beautiful, and noble, and your life will be a reflection of these things.

A calm mind is the fruit of wisdom. Calmness of mind is the result of the patient practice of self-control. I know few practices that will help you acquire this calmness of mind, heart, and spirit like the rosary will. And by learning to direct your thoughts toward God, you will learn to direct your life toward God.

In the rosary, we have twenty mysteries that beget twenty lessons in life, love, the attainment of virtue, and the genius of God's plan for humanity.

The Joyful Mysteries

The Annunciation: In the First Joyful Mystery we learn about the power of saying yes to God's will in our lives, as we witness Mary surrendering with her whole heart to God's designs for her life (cf. Luke 1:28–38). Fruit of the Mystery: Desire to do God's will.

The Visitation: In the Second Joyful Mystery we learn the value of service as Mary leaves her home to attend to her cousin Elizabeth (cf. Luke 1:39–42). Fruit of the Mystery: Humility.

The Birth of Jesus: In the Third Joyful Mystery we encounter the humility of Jesus, the Son of God, born in a stable (cf. Luke 2:1–7). Fruit of the Mystery: Detachment from the things of this world.

The Presentation: In the Fourth Joyful Mystery we witness a powerful example of obedience as Mary submits her child, the Son of God, to the Law of Moses (cf. Luke 2:23–32). Fruit of the Mystery: Obedience.

The Finding of Jesus in the Temple: In the Fifth Joyful Mystery we learn that true wisdom does not come from the mere attainment of knowledge; rather, it is a gift from God (cf. Luke 2:45–49). Fruit of the Mystery: Vocation & Evangelization.

The Luminous Mysteries

The Baptism of Jesus: In the First Luminous Mystery we hear the voice of the Father saying, "This is my beloved Son in whom I am well pleased," (Matthew 3:16–17) and we learn to stay close to the Father. Fruit of the Mystery: Openness to the Holy Spirit.

The Miracle at Cana: In the Second Luminous Mystery Jesus transforms water into wine (John 2:12) and we are reminded of his ability to transform our lives and the world. Fruit of the Mystery: Trust in God's Providence.

The Proclamation of the Kingdom: In the Third Luminous Mystery Jesus invites all people of all times to conversion—"Repent, for the Kingdom of God is at hand" (Mark 1:15)—and we ask to be filled with a desire for holiness. Fruit of the Mystery: Repentance.

The Transfiguration: In the Fourth Luminous Mystery we witness Jesus as he really is, the light of the world, and we ask for the spiritual courage to seek truth and light wherever it leads us (Luke 9:28–31). Fruit of the Mystery: Desire for Holiness.

The Institution of the Eucharist: The Fifth Luminous Mystery, in which Jesus teaches us how to love by holding nothing back, surrendering himself completely (John 6:51). Fruit of the Mystery: Love for the Eucharist.

The Sorrowful Mysteries

The Agony in the Garden: In the First Sorrowful Mystery we learn the importance of perseverance in prayer (cf. Luke 22:41–45). Fruit of the Mystery: Patience.

The Scourging at the Pillar: In the Second Sorrowful Mystery our spirits are renewed for the sacrifices of each day, and we learn never to despise the little things and the value of attention to detail (cf. John 19:1). Fruit of the Mystery: Self-Control.

The Crowning with Thorns: In the Third Sorrowful Mystery we learn compassion for those who are mocked and rejected, and we ask forgiveness for the times we have added to the insults of others (cf. Matthew 27:27–30). Fruit of the Mystery: Moral Courage.

The Carrying of the Cross: In the Fourth Sorrowful Mystery we are moved to help Jesus carry his cross by standing up to injustice and influencing our environment in a positive way (cf. John 19:17–18). Fruit of the Mystery: Desire to lay down our lives for others.

The Crucifixion: In the Fifth Sorrowful Mystery we experience the pain evil causes and feel the weight of our own sins (cf. Luke 23:42–46). Fruit of the Mystery: Surrender.

The Glorious Mysteries

The Resurrection: In the First Glorious Mystery we are reminded of the reality of life after death, and we learn to live with that in mind (cf. Mark 16:1–7). Fruit of the Mystery: Faith.

The Ascension: In the Second Glorious Mystery we are reminded of the great commission to continue the work of Jesus on earth by spreading the Gospel (cf. Mark 16:15–20). Fruit of the Mystery: Hope.

The Descent of the Holy Spirit: In the Third Glorious Mystery we are reminded that we are assisted in our efforts to do good by the unfathomable power of the Holy Spirit alive within us (cf. Acts 2:1–4). Fruit of the Mystery: Wisdom.

The Assumption: In the Fourth Glorious Mystery we are reminded of the beauty of purity of mind, body, spirit, and intention (cf. Revelation 12:1, 12:17). Fruit of the Mystery: Purity.

The Crowning of Mary Queen of Heaven: In the Fifth Glorious Mystery we learn to honor and seek the counsel of those who attain virtue in their lives (cf. Song of Songs 4:7–12). Fruit of the Mystery: Friendship with Mary.

These are twenty lessons worthy of constant reflection; twenty lessons that never cease to challenge us. I hope you will consider making this ancient spiritual exercise a part of your spiritual routines.

• More Than One Way •

There is more to praying the rosary than just saying the rosary. Anyone can say the rosary—just teach them the words and they can rattle them off. But to genuinely pray the rosary, we must have a clear objective in our minds. The rosary is not magic. There is no deal-making to be done with God. So many rosaries don't equal a prayer answered by God.

Prayer doesn't change God; prayer changes us. It is more rewarding to approach prayer seeking to understand God more, rather than seeing an opportunity to give God his instructions for the day. If we approach prayer with the hope of growing in virtue we will never be disappointed.

There are many different practical approaches to the rosary. The first is to focus on the words, which are deeply rooted in the Scriptures and Christian tradition. The Our Father was, of course, given to us by Jesus himself (cf. Matthew 6:9–13). The Creed represents the first expression of Christian conviction. The first part of the Hail Mary comes from the message delivered by the angel to Mary in Nazareth: "Hail, full of grace. The Lord is with thee." (Luke 1:28) This greeting is then followed by the words Elizabeth used to greet Mary during the Visitation: "Blessed art thou among women, and blessed is the fruit of thy womb." (Luke 1:42) The Glory Be is the simplest expression of Christian praise and belief in the triune God.

And from the times of antiquity, Christians have placed themselves under the name of God and the sign of redemption, thus giving us the Sign of the Cross.

The words of the rosary are powerful and filled with meaning, but so are the mysteries that we use as a backdrop to each decade.

One thing is certain: Your mind cannot do two things at once. This is where many people become discouraged with praying the rosary. They try to pray the words and meditate on the mystery at the same time. Impossible! We must decide between the two.

On those occasions when you choose to meditate on the mysteries, allow the words to float by. Get lost in the scene. Imagine yourself there. When you choose to focus on the words, it may help to meditate on the mystery for a few moments before each decade.

I also find it very fruitful to identify an intention with each decade. Offering each decade for a person or a situation helps me to stay focused, and avails me the opportunity to pray for many people in my life.

There are some people who think that we should pray the rosary every day. In my own life, there have been months, even years, when I have prayed the rosary every day. At other times, I have gone weeks and months without praying the rosary. Generally, I have discovered that when I make time for this simple but profound practice of prayer I am a better person. When I have the discipline to pray the rosary regularly I seem to have a certain calmness and awareness, which makes me more readily disposed to living a life of virtue.

I don't think we need to enter the debate of whether or not every Catholic should pray the rosary every day. I do, however, think that all Catholics should be able to bring forth the rosary from their spiritual storehouse from time to time as the Spirit prompts them.

Our prayer lives should be dynamic, like love. Our love should be constant, but it may express itself in many different ways at different times. So it is with prayer. Learn to allow the Spirit to guide you to the type of prayer that will most benefit you on a particular day—not the type of prayer you "feel like" doing, but the type of prayer that will most benefit you on that day, depending on the disposition of your soul.

• The Real Objection •

I suspect the real reason modern Catholics don't have a more passionate relationship with the rosary is because, in general, I don't think we are comfortable with the role Mary plays in our spirituality. For hundreds of years, our non-Catholic Christian brothers and sisters have been accusing us of worshipping Mary and the saints, and I don't think we have done a good job of settling this question.

Do Catholics worship Mary and the saints? No. We pray to them but not to worship them, and not in the same way we pray to God. Think of it in this way: If you got sick and asked me to pray for you, I would. This does not make me uniquely Catholic, or even uniquely Christian. There are many non-Christians who believe in the power of prayer. If I ask my non-Catholic Christian friends whether they pray for their spouse or their children, they will say yes. If I ask them to pray for me, they will say yes. This is the same principle. We believe that Mary and the saints are dead to this world, but we also believe they live on in the next world. And we believe that their prayers are just as powerful—even more powerful. We are essentially saying to them, "We have problems down here. You know what it is like because you have been here; pray for us!"

Our non-Catholic Christian friends don't believe people can still pray in the afterlife. We do. Our spiritual universe is just bigger. In fact, one of the most incredible things about our Catholic faith is the vastness of our spiritual universe.

• Mary •

Mary is the most famous woman in history. She leads all prominent women who have earned their fame by living a life of virtue. She has inspired more art and music than any other woman in history, and even in the modern age, she fascinates the imaginations of men and women of all faiths. In our own age, Mary has appeared on the cover of *Time* magazine more often than any other person.

I suspect that if we are to reconcile the great disharmony that exists between the role of men and the role of women in modern society we will need the insight of this great feminine role model. Is it possible for us to understand the dignity, value, mystery, and wonder of women, without first understanding this woman?

But beyond her fame and her historical importance is her centrality to Christian life. The first Christians gathered around her for comfort and guidance, yet some modern Catholics treat her like she has some contagious disease. One of the great challenges that we face as modern Catholics is to find a genuine place for Mary in our spirituality.

My wife recently gave birth to our first child, a son. Being a father has filled me with many new spiritual insights. I love this little boy so much and if I can love him so much in all my brokenness and with all my limitations, how much more God must love me. Through my son I have experienced the love of God in a whole new way. I also just yearn to be with him. When I am on the road, or even at the office for the day, I yearn to get home and hold him, play with him, be with him. It strikes me that perhaps above everything else God just yearns to be with us.

The birth of our son has also renewed my relationship with Mary. It has occurred to me that no matter how much I love my son, my wife will always have a unique perspective on his life. It doesn't mean that she loves him more or that I love him less. It just means that a mother sees her child's life in a way that nobody else can. If I don't take time occasionally to ask her about this motherly perspective I unnecessarily miss a part of my son's life.

A mother has a unique perspective. Nobody sees the life of a child the way the child's mother does—not even the father. This is Mary's perspective of Jesus' life. It seems to me that every genuine Christian, not just Catholics, should be interested in that perspective—and not just interested, but fascinated. In the rosary we ponder the life of Jesus through the eyes of his mother. This is an incredibly powerful experience if we enter into it fully.

Conclusion

Life is difficult. Every day we face a new problem. We can accept that or get aggravated, but we cannot change it. The problem isn't that life is difficult. It is supposed to be difficult. The problem is that we expect it to be easy or we try to make it easy.

Life proposes a series of challenges, dilemmas, problems, dissatisfactions, heartaches, and opportunities. How we respond to these events determines the direction and quality of our lives.

But we spend so much time and energy trying to avoid life's difficulties rather than facing them head-on. All our efforts to avoid the difficulties of life lead us away from everything that is deeply satisfying. If your goal was an easy life, would any of the following be possible? Meaningful relationships, deeply satisfying work, health and vitality, raising children, starting a business, or mastery of a profession or hobby?

Human beings are at their best when they face the difficulties of life head-on. We learn to delay gratification, embrace reality, release illusions, accept responsibility for our lives, and live in the wisdom that the most satisfying experiences are often difficult.

The difficulties of life help us grow spiritually, but we need a vibrant spiritual life to deal with life's problems.

The Seven Pillars of Catholic Spirituality are a spiritual toolkit that will help you develop a dynamic relationship with God and a vibrant spirituality. Commit yourself to adding one of these powerful spiritual practices to your life each week for the next seven weeks and you will be amazed at the many ways they enrich your life.

Week One: Daily Prayer

Visit your church for 10 minutes each day and talk to God about what is on your heart and mind.

Week Two: The Bible

Read one chapter of the Gospels each day.

+ Spend 10 minutes each day in conversational prayer.

Week Three: The Mass

Choose a weekday and attend Mass.

+ Read one chapter of the Gospels each day.

+ Spend 10 minutes each day in conversational prayer.

Week Four: Spiritual Reading

Read 5 pages of a spiritual book each day.

+ Choose a weekday and attend Mass.

+ Read one chapter of the Gospels each day.

+ Spend 10 minutes each day in conversational prayer.

Week Five: Fasting

Say no to your body once a day and fast on Friday. What does a fast consist of? One full meal, two smaller meals that together do not equal the full meal, and no eating between meals.

+ Read 5 pages of a spiritual book each day.

+ Choose a weekday and attend Mass.

+ Read one chapter of the Gospels each day.

+ Spend 10 minutes each day in conversational prayer.

Week Six: The Rosary

Pray the rosary each day. Or begin with one decade each day and let it evolve from there.

+ Say no to your body once a day and fast on Friday.

+ Read 5 pages of a spiritual book each day.

+ Choose a weekday and attend Mass.

+ Read one chapter of the Gospels each day.

+ Spend 10 minutes each day in conversational prayer.

Week Seven: Confession

Go to Confession this week. If you haven't participated in the sacrament for a while, you may want to make an appointment to see a priest. Commit yourself to going to Confession once a month.

+ Pray the rosary each day. Or begin with one decade each day and let it evolve from there.

+ Say no to your body once a day and fast on Friday.

+ Read 5 pages of a spiritual book each day.

+ Choose a weekday and attend Mass.

+ Read one chapter of the Gospels each day.

+ Spend 10 minutes each day in conversational prayer.

Every Week and Beyond. . .

Spend 10 minutes each day in conversational prayer.

Read one chapter of the Gospels each day.

Choose a weekday and attend Mass.

Read 5 pages of a spiritual book each day.

Say no to your body once a day and fast on Friday.

Pray the rosary each day.

Go to Confession once a month.

Outside of attending Mass once during the week and participating in Confession once a month, these spiritual practices will require less than forty-five minutes a day. But if adding one each week seems overwhelming, you could add one every two weeks, or once a month.

Remember. . . a tree with deep roots can weather any storm. The storms of life are inevitable. It's not a question of whether or not there will be another storm. The question is: When will the next storm get here? And when the next storm gets here, it's too late to sink the roots. When the next storm gets here, you either have the roots or you don't.

The Seven Pillars of Catholic Spirituality: It's time to sink these roots deep into your life.

G.K. Chesterton observed, "Christianity has not been tried and found wanting. It has been found difficult and left untried."

Don't let it be left untried in your life.

Notes

Notes

Notes

Notes

Notes

Notes

Notes